Embroidered Quilts

From Hands and Hearts

By Christina DeArmond, Eula Lang and Kaye Spitzli

Embroidered Quilts
From Hands and Hearts

By Christina DeArmond, Eula Lang and Kaye Spitzli

Editor: Deb Rowden
Designer: Kelly Ludwig
Photography: Aaron T. Leimkuehler
Illustration: Lon Eric Craven
Technical Editor: Kathe Dougherty
Production assistance: Jo Ann Groves

Published by:
Kansas City Star Books
1729 Grand Blvd.
Kansas City, Missouri, USA 64108

First edition, first printing
ISBN: 978-1-933466-79-8

Library of Congress Control Number: 2008932755

Printed in the United States of America by Walsworth
Publishing Co., Marceline, MO

To order copies, call StarInfo at (816) 234-4636 and say
"Books."

 KANSAS CITY STAR BOOKS

The Quilter's Home Page

www.PickleDish.com

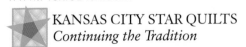
KANSAS CITY STAR QUILTS
Continuing the Tradition

Contents

Dedication

We dedicate this book to our fathers, Rex Slankard, Francis Scranton and Leland "Pete" Lawson. We honor their influence and love in our lives. During the writing of this book, all three of them underwent health issues and Francis went home to be with the Lord. Their influence is with us every day and we honor them for their strong and loving leadership in their families.

Acknowledgements

We thank all those who were so supportive and helpful to us in the writing of this book. First of all our wonderful husbands Bill DeArmond, Rob Lang and John Spitzli for putting up with late night edit sessions and lack of home-cooked meals. Thank you to Deb Rowden for her good-natured nudging. We extend our great appreciation to Aaron T. Leimkuehler for his excellent photography and attention to detail. To Doug Weaver, Kelly Ludwig and the rest of The Kansas City Star staff for being such a great organization to work with. Thank you to Arlene Lawson for her many hours of embroidery and binding work. Thank you to Nan Doljac for letting us photograph Flit and Flutter and to Shannon Slagle for making the Calendar Throw Pillows. Thank you to the rest of the employees of Quilting Bits & Pieces and the Wednesday morning ladies for their encouragement and support.

About the Authors

Christina DeArmond, Eula Lang and Kaye Spitzli are friends, avid quilters and business partners. As co-owners of Quilting Bits & Pieces Quilt Shop in Eudora, Kansas and pattern company Of One Mind, they especially enjoy appliqué and embroidery and usually incorporate them into their quilt designs.

Planning *Embroidered Quilts: From Hands and Hearts* led them to reminisce about their own embroidery history. They all noticed that embroidery is often a young girl's introduction into the world of sewing. This was true for all of them. They share their early embroidery memories:

the '70s), doing crewelwork and counted cross stitch. Now most of my embroidery efforts are aimed at adding touches or blocks to my quilts."

Kaye

"I have childhood memories of embroidered pillowcases (that would leave a cute print on my cheek if I slept on the pillowcase just right), embroidered dresser scarves and tea towels. In the evenings when mom would do her 'handwork'—which often included embroidery—I remember working on stamped designs alongside her. As a young mother, my first quilt was blocks of embroidered barnyard animals for our first child. Beyond that, embroidery was only used to embellish clothes I made for my daughters or counted cross stitch. More recently I've used a few embroidery stitches to accent appliqué designs. Working on quilts for this book has been a trip down memory lane and a reminder of just how relaxing and fun embroidery can be."

Christina

"I remember my mom standing over the ironing board, even on hot summer days, pressing our pillowcases. The pillowcases were always embroidered, along with tablecloths, and tea towels. Mom worked out in the fields plowing, planting, and harvesting, then came in and worked on dinner. In her 'spare' time in the evenings, she would sit and embroider. I'm not sure she has ever used a tea towel that didn't have embroidery on it. Mom embroidered tea towels for each of her children and grandchildren as they married and started their

new homes. I don't remember my mother teaching me to embroider, I just know I always knew how and I'm sure it's because she taught me. I enjoy doing embroidery and I love how it dresses up a quilt block, adding details and depth."

Eula

"When I was five or so I recall wanting to embroider, so my mom drew a poodle on a piece of red cloth. I embroidered it with white thread (reverse red work!). I recall thinking it took a very long time to complete. How fun it would be to have that piece now to look at but I have no idea whatever became of it. As the years went on, I enjoyed embroidering flowers on my jeans (remember

Antique Redwork Quilts, Our Inspiration

As we prepared to write this book about embroidery on quilts, a good friend sent us two antique redwork quilts for inspirational purposes. There were so many fun blocks that we decided to share some of them with you, along with some of our original ones.

All three of us instantly fell in love with the calendar blocks, there were also a lot of lovely floral blocks. To make use of these blocks, we came up with different settings to showcase them.

In the projects that follow, you will find the floral blocks in the Russet Bouquet and the calendar blocks are interchangeable between the Russet Bouquet, All Seasons Turn Sage, Times and Seasons and Calendar wallhangings so feel free to create your own quilt by mixing and matching the blocks and settings. These blocks will fit a square that is 7" finished or larger. Here are the two antique quilts.

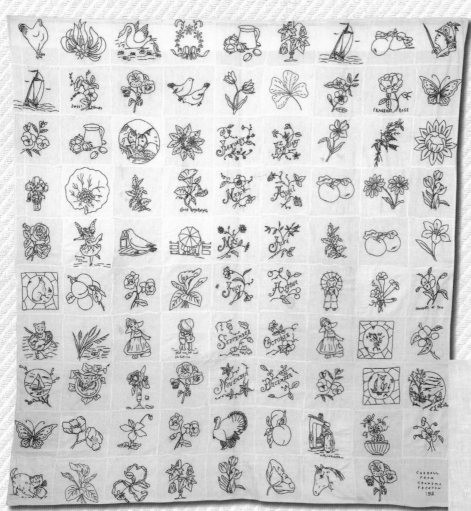

This quilt from the collection of Eula Lang served as inspiration for several quilts in this book. It contains a wealth of old patterns. The origin of the quilt is unknown, but the corner block contains some information about it (see the detail photo).

CARROLL FROM GRANDMA PRESTON 1918

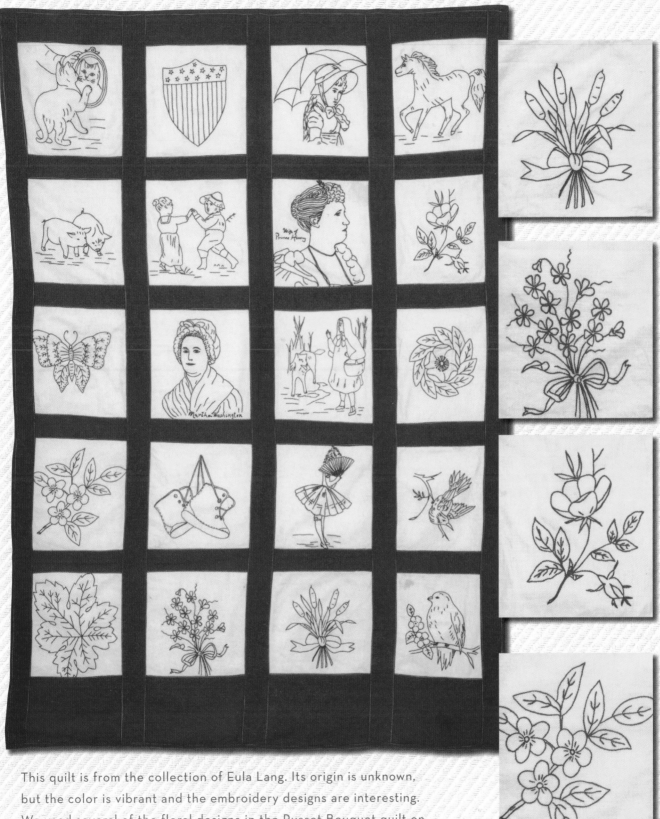

This quilt is from the collection of Eula Lang. Its origin is unknown, but the color is vibrant and the embroidery designs are interesting. We used several of the floral designs in the Russet Bouquet quilt on page 16.

Embroidery – A Brief History

By Christina DeArmond

Hand embroidery is an art passed down from generation to generation. *Quilts in America* defines it as "enriching a flat foundation by working into it with a needle, colored silks and wools, gold or silver threads, and other extraneous material in floral, geometrical or figure designs." Embroidery and quilting are art forms that compliment each other. Embroidery can be used to enhance a quilt or it can be the main focus of a quilt. Its use in quilts has changed through history and continues to adapt to new trends.

We can trace the history of American embroidery back to the early settlers. Children (boys and girls) were taught to sew as early as they could hold a needle and thread to help their mother with the household sewing. As girls grew older, they were taught basic embroidery stitches to embellish their clothing and to make quilts for their hope chests. The stem stitch, satin stitch, chain stitch, knotted stitches and crosses are a few of the stitches that have survived throughout history.

As immigrants arrived, they brought skills learned in their old country, although they had to adapt to the limited supplies available in the original colonies. While the American colonies were being settled, needlework in England still consisted mainly of teaching young girls their alphabet and numbers by making samplers. Learning to make precise stitches was important and it was also a sign of wealth, as only the wealthy had time to sit and practice their stitches.

Whitework

Because of the importance placed on handwork, one of the early trends in early America was "white work". White work was simply white embroidery on a white background. It was done in all weights of thread, from silk to wool. White work decorated household linens and accessories, and it held up well to frequent and vigorous washing. White bedspreads were also decorated with many types of embroidery stitches, particularly French knots and bullion knots.

The art of forming knots to make a design is a form of embroidery called candlewicking. Entire coverlet surfaces were decorated with French knots and bullions. Knot sizes varied according to the strands of thread used. These coverlets included many other basic embroidery stitches such as the satin stitch, backstitch, stem stitch, couching, and outline stitch.

Patched quilts

Patchwork quilts started gaining in popularity after 1840 when the manufacture of textiles moved to being factory based. They were often made as a matter of necessity rather than style. Quilts were needed to survive the cold, harsh winters and tended to be very practical. Scraps of cloth and old clothing that could no longer be repaired or re-made as part of a different piece of clothing were used to make quilts. If the fabric was not good enough for use in a quilt top, it was used as stuffing in the middle of the quilt. This type of quilt was looked down upon by the English, who were more concerned about their needlework skills.

Although these bed quilts were an essential part of many American households, as late as 1875 they were still not appreciated. According to *Household Magazine*, the admonishment is clear that "the unsightly covering known as the patched quilt should not be seen on a bed." Several articles suggesting ways to raise standards of housekeeping rejected traditional calico patchwork in favor of decorative embroidery.

Baltimore Album Quilts

Baltimore album style quilts were very popular during the mid 1800s in America. These quilts featured intricate appliqué blocks with many details. Embroidery was used to outline and emphasize details such as stems, stamens, flower petals and leaves; or beaks, eyes, and tails of birds on appliqué blocks. Writing on some of the blocks also was done in embroidery. The details in these blocks would not have been as vivid had it not been for the embroidery.

Signed quilts

Signing quilts was commonly done by embroidering names, dates, locations, and sometimes even brief descriptions. The placement of the signature could be anywhere on the quilt. Sometimes it was quite prominent—even a focal point—and on other quilts it would be placed where it was barely visible.

Signing and dating the quilt or linens was also important so they could be kept in the proper rotation. Due to the harsh laundering soaps, quilts and linens needed to be rotated so they would not wear out too quickly.

Signature quilts became popular in the 1860s. During the Civil War, quilts were used for fund-raisers for the Red Cross and other charities. For a donation of a few pennies, one could embroider their name on a block or directly onto a quilt. When the quilt was completed, it was raffled or sold to the highest bidder. Most of these quilts were done in red, as red dyes were the most colorfast.

Redwork

In addition to making fund-raising quilts, during the late 19th century women were also stitching redwork quilts for their homes. Redwork is embroidery stitched completely in red thread. Outline embroidery or "etching on linen" was also done in blue and green, but they never gained as much popularity as red.

Redwork quilts were a refreshing change from the heavy Victorian crazy quilts. Patterns became commercially available in all types of designs. The most popular designs were Kate Greenaway designs of girls in bonnets with umbrellas, watering cans, and fans. Historical figures, botanical prints, and anything to do with the Orient were also in demand. The popularity of redwork continued through the 1920s and 1930s, when it had more of a childlike appeal. Sunbonnet Sue, nursery rhymes, fairy tales, barnyard figures, pets, state flowers and birds were all popular designs for redwork quilts.

Penny squares became very popular during the 1930s. Penny squares were squares of muslin with designs already traced on them. They could be purchased to embroider and/or collect for only a penny or two. Most were stitched in red. Redwork stayed popular until the 1940s, when women went to work outside the home to support the war cause. It made a comeback in the late 1990s and is still popular today.

Still popular

Embroidery continues to be popular today. Part of its uniqueness is that a quilt can be designed around the embroidery or the embroidery can be used to enhance the piecing or appliqué of the quilt. However it is used, the end result is always wonderful.

Recommended reading

Quilts in America by Patsy and Myron Orlofsky, McGraw Hill Publishing Company, New York, NY 1974.
America's Quilts and Coverlets by Carleton L. Safford and Robert Bishop, Weathervane Books, 1974.
The American Quilt Story by Susan Jenkins and Linda Seward, Rodale Press, 1992.

All Seasons Turn Sage

60" x 60" • **Embroidered block size: 9" x 9"**

Pieced and embroidered by Christina DeArmond

Quilted by Eula Lang

Embroidery patterns for this quilt are on pages 109-120.

I've always loved quilts with many small pieces and I also enjoy embroidering. So I combined the two and came up with All Seasons Turn Sage. I used the monthly blocks from the antique quilt on page 4 and stitched them on a pieced background. It is important to have subtle color changes in the background blocks so that the embroidery is the main focus, not the piecing. It is also a little challenging to trace the embroidered blocks through the seams on the pieced background. Using light colors for the background piecing along with a light box will help. It may be a little more challenging to trace, but the effect is well worth it. The subtle changes make for a beautiful quilt.

Fabric requirements/supplies

This pattern uses several very similar fabrics—we have identified them as A, B, C and so on. Please label your fabrics with the letters below.

For the embroidery blocks:
- ♥ Three different neutrals (A, B, and C) – 1/2 yard of each
- ♥ A fourth neutral (D) – 2/3 yard

For the alternate blocks:
- ♥ Three sage prints (E, F and G) – 1 1/4 yards of each
- ♥ Plum accent (H) for the alternate blocks and border - 7/8 yard
- ♥ Binding: 5/8 yard

- ♥ Embroidery floss:
  - ❖ Plum – 4 skeins
  - ❖ Sage – 2 skeins
- ♥ Pigma pen 01 brown
- ♥ Embroidery needle size 7

Cutting instructions

Label the fabric strips with their appropriate letter (A, B, and so on) as you cut them.

Pieced embroidery blocks:
- ♥ Nine - 1 1/2" x width of the fabric (wof) strips from each of A, B, & C
- ♥ Three - 3 1/2" x wof strips from D, cross cut every 1 1/2" to make 72 - 1 1/2" x 3 1/2" rectangles

Pieced alternate blocks:
- ♥ Nine - 1 1/2" x wof strips from each of E, F, and G
- ♥ Three - 3 1/2" x wof strips from H, cross cut every 1 1/2" to make 78 - 1 1/2" x 3 1/2" rectangles

Inner pieced border:
- ♥ Eleven - 1" x wof strips from H
- ♥ Six - 1" x wof strips from D

Outer pieced border:
- ♥ Thirteen - 1 1/2" x wof strips from each of E, F, and G

Binding:
- ♥ Seven - 2 1/2" strips

Piecing the embroidery block units

1. Using the 1 1/2" A, B and C strips, sew an A strip to a B strip along the long side. Sew a C strip to the AB strip set in the same manner. The B strip needs to be between the A and C strips. Press the seams toward the C strip. This is an ABC strip set unit. Make 2 more for a total of 3 ABC strip set units.

WOF

1 1/2"	A
1 1/2"	B
1 1/2"	C

2. Make 3 ACB strip set units as in step 1. Press the seams toward the A strips.

WOF

1 1/2"	A
1 1/2"	C
1 1/2"	B

3. Make 3 BAC strip set units as in step 1. Press the seams toward the A strips.

WOF

1 1/2"	B
1 1/2"	A
1 1/2"	C

For embroidery
Use 2 strands embroidery floss or 1 strand 16 weight Perle cotton unless otherwise noted.

4. Cross cut the strip sets every 3 1/2" until you have 24 - 3 1/2" pieced squares from EACH combination of strip sets for a total of 72 - 3 1/2" pieced squares.

3 1/2" 3 1/2" 3 1/2" 3 1/2" → Continue

5. From each of the 3 strip set units (ABC, ACB and BAC) cross cut 12 - 1 1/2" units. These 36 units measure 1 1/2" x 3 1/2".

1 1/2"   1 1/2"   1 1/2"

Abbreviations
- corner setting triangles=cst
- half-square triangles=hst
- side setting triangles=sst
- width of fabric=wof

Assembling the embroidery blocks

Make 12

The block is constructed by sewing the strip set units and the accent strips into rows, then attaching the rows. The strips in the strip set units will run horizontally in each finished block. Two of each strip set combination will be used for each block, randomly placed within each block. Assemble as described below:

Top row: 1 1/2" x 3 1/2" pieced strip, strip D, 3 1/2" pieced square, strip D, 3 1/2" pieced square

Middle row: 3 1/2" pieced square, strip D, 3 1/2" pieced square, strip D, 1 1/2" x 3 1/2" pieced strip

Bottom row: 1 1/2" x 3 1/2" pieced strip, Strip D, 3 1/2" pieced square, strip D, 3 1/2" pieced square

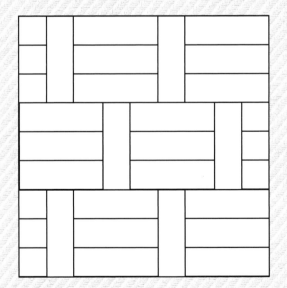

Piecing the alternate block units

1. Following the method used in Step 1 of Piecing the embroidery block units on page 12, make 3 EFG strip set units. Press the seams toward the G strips.

2. Make 3 EGF strip set units. Press the seams toward the E strips.

3. Make 3 FEG strip set units. Press the seams towards the E strips.

4. Cross cut these strip sets every 3 1/2" until you have 26 - 3 1/2" pieced squares from each combination of strip sets for a total of 78 - 3 1/2" pieced squares.

5. From each of these 3 strip set units, cross cut 13 - 1 1/2" units. These 39 units measure 1 1/2" x 3 1/2".

Assembling the alternate blocks

Make 13

The block is now constructed by arranging the strip set units and the accent strip into rows, then attaching the rows. The strips in the strip set units will run horizontally in each finished block. Two of each strip set combination will be used for each block, randomly placed within each block. Assemble as described below:

Top row: 1 1/2" x 3 1/2" pieced strip, strip H, 3 1/2" pieced square, strip H, 3 1/2" pieced square

Middle row: 3 1/2" pieced square, strip H, 3 1/2" pieced square, strip H, 1 1/2" x 3 1/2" pieced strip

Bottom row: 1 1/2" x 3 1/2" pieced strip, strip H, 3 1/2" pieced square, strip H, 3 1/2" pieced square

Embroidery

Note: A light box is great for tracing.

1. Trace the selected design onto clean white paper, using a heavy black marker, or make a copy using a copy machine.

2. Tape the copied design onto a light box and then tape the pieced neutral block over it. Rotate some blocks 180 degrees, but make sure piece D is vertical.

3. Trace the design using a Pigma pen.

4. Using 2 strands of embroidery floss, stem stitch over all the traced lines.

5. Fill in the wide openings of the capital letters with a satin stitch, using 3 strands of embroidery floss.

6. Embroider all 12 blocks.

Quilt assembly

1. Assemble the quilt as shown in the diagram, making sure pieces D and H are vertical. For variety, rotate some blocks 180 degrees.

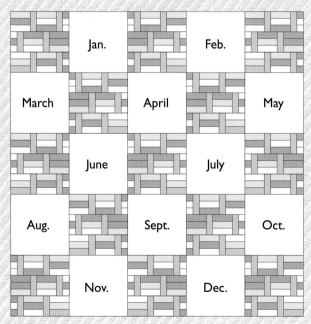

Assembly diagram

2. Press the seams toward the alternate pieced blocks.

3. Sew the 1" H strips together at the short ends. Cut two 1" x 45 1/2" strips. Sew one to each side of the quilt.

4. Cut two 1" x 46 1/2" H strips. Sew one to the top and one to the bottom of the quilt.

5. Sew the 1" D strips together at the short ends. Cut two 1" x 46 1/2" strips and sew one to each side of the quilt.

6. Cut two 1" x 47 1/2" D strips. Sew one to the top and one to the bottom of the quilt.

7. Cut two 1" x 47 1/2" strips from the H strip you made in step 3. Sew one to each side of the quilt.

8. Cut two 1" x 48 1/2" H strips. Sew one to the top and one to the bottom of the quilt.

Outer border

1. Make 5 EFG strip set units as described in step 1 of piecing instructions for alternate blocks.

2. Make 4 EGF strip set units as described in step 2 of piecing instructions for alternate blocks.

3. Make 4 FEG strip set units as described in step 3 of piecing instructions for alternate blocks.

4. Cross cut the strip sets every 3 1/2". You need a total of 144 of these units. You will get 143 out of these strip set units, so you will need to make one from some of the extra units that went into the center of the quilt or make one additional strip set unit.

5. Make 36 four-patch blocks by combining 4 of these units, twisting them so that a vertical one goes next to a horizontal one.

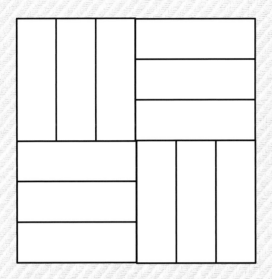

6. Connect 8 of these four-patch blocks for each side border of the quilt being careful of the placement so that the vertical strips are at the top left of each border.

7. Connect 10 of the four-patch blocks for the top and bottom borders of the quilt. Sew one to the top and repeat for the bottom of the quilt. Be careful with the placement of these: the vertical strips are on the top left corners of these borders.

Finishing

1. Layer with backing and batting and quilt as desired.

2. Bind, using the seven 2 1/2" strips.

Russet Bouquet

57 1/2" x 72 1/2"
Embroidered block size: 7" x 7"
Pieced by Eula Lang, embroidered by Arlene Lawson and Eula Lang,
quilted by Eula Lang

Embroidery patterns for this quilt are on pages 71-82.

Our two antique quilts included such a beautiful selection of floral blocks, I designed a setting to showcase twelve of them. I love using colors that are warm and vibrant. In this quilt, I chose to contrast the warm russet tones with the visually cooler teal. I had fun playing with the secondary pattern created by the placement of the various background colors. The embroidery work is a simple stem stitch and the 7" finished size will also work with the calendar blocks. Have fun with it!

Fabric requirements/supplies

- ♥ Cream – 3/4 yard
- ♥ Russet – 2/3 yard (A)
- ♥ Two different brown/teal prints – 2/3 yard each (B and C)
- ♥ Brown – 2/3 yard (D)
- ♥ Cream print – 7/8 yard (CP)
- ♥ Teal - 1 1/4 yards (T)
- ♥ Teal/brown print for the border and binding – 2 yards
- ♥ Teal perle cotton size 16 – 1 ball
- ♥ Embroidery needle size 7

Cutting instructions

From the cream fabric cut:

- ♥ Twelve - 8 1/2" squares

From EACH of A, B, C and D cut:

- ♥ Six - 5 7/8" squares. Cut these in half diagonally to make 12 triangles.
- ♥ Twelve - 3 3/8" squares. Cut these in half diagonally to make 24 triangles.
- ♥ Twenty-four - 3 " squares

From the cream print cut:

- ♥ Forty-eight - 3" squares
- ♥ Fourteen- 3" x 5 1/2" rectangles
- ♥ Fourteen - 3 3/8" squares. Cut these in half diagonally to make 28 triangles.

From the teal fabric cut:

- ♥ Thirty-four - 3" x 5 1/2" rectangles
- ♥ Thirty-four-3 3/8" squares. Cut these in half diagonally to make 68 triangles
- ♥ Six - 1 3/4" x width of fabric (wof) strips for the inner border

From the teal/brown print cut LENGTHWISE:

- ♥ Two - 5 1/2" x 63" strips for the side borders
- ♥ Two - 5 1/2" x 58" strips for the top and bottom borders
- ♥ Four - 2 1/2 x length of fabric (lof) strips for the binding

Embroidery

1. Trace one floral pattern onto each of the twelve 8 1/2" cream squares, centering the design on the block. Be careful with the placement so the floral pattern is on point.

2. Embroider all 12 blocks with the stem stitch. See pages 63-67 for embroidery instructions. Press the blocks by placing them right side down on a soft surface.

3. Trim each block to 7 1/2" square, keeping the design centered on the block.

Block piecing

1. Sew one of the A 5 7/8" triangles to the upper left side of an embroidered square. Match the center of the long side of the triangle with the center of the side of the square. The points of the triangle will extend just a little beyond the square at the corner (see diagram below). Repeat this process with the 11 remaining squares. Press the seams toward the triangles.

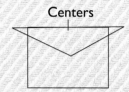

Centers

2. Continue sewing the 5 7/8" triangles to the embroidered squares until you have one each of the A, B, C and D triangles sewn to each embroidered square. Place the B triangles on the upper right side, the C triangles on the lower left and the D triangles on the lower right. Be careful to keep the color placement the same on every block.

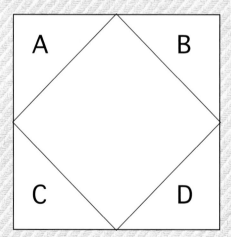

Block Assembly

Flying geese units

1. Make the flying geese units by placing a 3" square on the corner of a 3" x 5 1/2" rectangle (see step 9 for color placement). Sew from corner to corner diagonally on the square as shown above right.

2. Trim the outer corner as shown below.

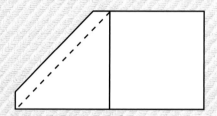

3. Press the seam toward the darker fabric. Repeat on the opposite corner to form a flying geese unit.

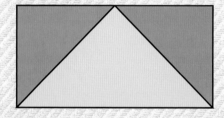

4. Make a total of 48 flying geese units in these color combinations:

From the 14 cream print (CP) rectangles make:

3 - A-CP-B

4 - B-CP-D

3 - C-CP-D

4 - A-CP-C

From the 34 teal (T) rectangles make:

8 - B-T-D

8 - A-T-C

9 - C-T-D

9 - A-T-B

Half-square triangle units

5. Sew 96 half-square triangle (hst) units in these color combinations.

7 - A-CP

7 - B-CP

7 - C-CP

7 - D-CP

17 - A-T

17 - B-T

17 - C-T

17 – D-T

To make the hsts, pair the 3 3/8" A, B, C and D triangles with the 3 3/8" T and CP triangles. Place them right sides together and stitch along the long side. Press the seam toward the darker fabrics.

6. Sew the hst units to each end of the flying geese units, matching the colors to the flying geese unit.

Example – you will have eight color combinations

7. Sew these strips to each side of the embroidery block units, matching the colors that touch and referring to the photo on page 16 for color placement. The CP units all will be on the exterior rows of the quilt and the T units on the interior.

Assembly diagram

8. Sew a 3" cream square to each end of the remaining flying geese/hst strips. Sew these strips to the top and bottom of each block, referring to the photo for color placement.

Quilt Assembly

Sew the blocks into rows, then sew the rows together referring to the photo for color placement.

Borders

1. Sew the ends of the 1 3/4" teal strips together to form one long strip. Cut two 60 1/2" long strips. Sew these strips to each side of the quilt. Cut two 48" long strips. Sew these strips to the top and bottom of the quilt.

2. Sew the 63" borders to each side of the quilt. Sew the 58" borders to the top and bottom of the quilt.

Finishing

1. Quilt as desired.

2. Bind with the 2 1/2" border fabric strips.

Times and Seasons

36 1/2" x 36 1/2"
Embroidered block size: 7" x 7"
Pieced by Eula Lang, embroidered by Arlene Lawson, quilted by Eula Lang

Embroidery patterns for this quilt are on pages 109–120.

Embroidered quilts—stitched with red floss, using red and white fabrics—are such a classic. Drawing on the inspiration of the two antique red work quilts, I felt it only appropriate that we should include a setting done in this traditional color scheme. The center block reminds me of both a clock and a mariner's compass, both of which serve as guides: one in time and the other in space. The quilt's name, Times and Seasons, reminds me of this symbolism.

Fabric requirements/supplies

- ♥ Cream - 7/8 yard
- ♥ Cream/red print - 2/3 yard
- ♥ Red print - 1 1/2 yards
- ♥ Red 16 weight perle cotton
- ♥ Embroidery needle size 7

Cutting Instructions

From the cream fabric cut:

- ♥ Twelve - 8 1/2" squares

From the cream/red print cut:

- ♥ Four- 1" squares
- ♥ Four pieces from corner template A pattern (see page 69)
- ♥ Use this fabric to paper piece the parts of the arcs marked white.

From the red print fabric cut:

- ♥ Twelve - 1" x 7 1/2" strips
- ♥ Four - 1" x 15" strips
- ♥ One center block circle template B (see page 70)

- ♥ Two - 4" x 30" strips
- ♥ Two - 4" x 37" strips
- ♥ Four - 2 1/2" x width of fabric strips
- ♥ Use this fabric to paper piece the parts of the arcs marked "red".

Sewing instructions

1. Trace one month pattern onto each of the twelve 8 1/2" square cream blocks, centering the design on the block.

2. Embroider all 12 blocks with the stem stitch for the main design, filling in the open parts of the capital letters with the satin stitch. See pages 63-67 for embroidery instructions. Press the blocks by placing them right side down on a soft surface.

3. Trim each block to 7 1/2" square, keeping the design centered on the block.

4. Make 7 copies of the paper pieced arc pattern on page 69.

5. Paper piece the arcs, placing the red fabric in the sections marked "red" and the cream/red print in the sections marked "white". Trim the sections on the marked line (not on the stitching line). Sew all 7 sections together to form a ring.

6. Sew the center circle cut from template B to the inside of this ring. To do this, fold both pieces in half vertically, then again horizontally and mark these divisions with pins. Match up the pins on both sections and continue pinning, easing in the fullness. Sew together.

7. Sew the 4 corner template A pieces together on the short sides. This will form a square with a large hole in the center. Press the seams open.

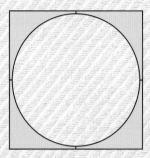

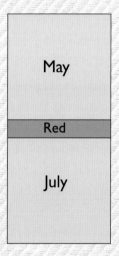

8. Sew this square to the circle unit. To do this, fold both pieces in half vertically, then again horizontally and mark these divisions with pins. Match up the pins on both sections and continue pinning easing in the fullness. Sew together.

Quilt assembly

1. Assemble and stitch the top row: January block, 1" x 7 1/2" strip, February block, 1" x 7 1/2" strip, March block, 1" x 7 1/2" strip, April block. Press the seams toward the red strips.

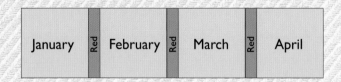

2. Sew a 1" x 7 1/2" strip to the bottom of the May block, then sew the top of the July block to the strip. Press the seams toward the red strips.

3. Sew a 1" x 7 1/2" strip to the bottom of the June block, then sew the top of the August block to the strip. Press the seams toward the red strips.

4. Assemble and stitch the middle section: May/July unit, 1" x 15" strip, center block, 1" x 15" strip, June/August unit. Press the seams toward the red strips.

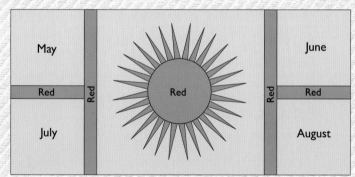

5. Assemble and stitch the bottom row: September block, 1" x 7 1/2" strip, October block, 1" x 7 1/2" strip, November block, 1" x 7 1/2" strip, December block. Press the seams toward the red strips.

Red/cream print   Red/cream print

Red   Red   Red

6. Make a sashing strip by sewing together the following pieces along the 1" sides: 1" x 7 1/2" strip, 1" cream/red square, 1" x 15" strip, 1" cream/red square, 1" x 7 1/2" strip. Press the seams toward the red strips. Repeat so you have 2 sashing strips.

7. Sew a sashing strip to the bottom of top row and the bottom of the middle section. Sew the middle section to the top row/sashing strip unit. Sew on the bottom row.

Borders/finishing

1. Sew the 4"x 30" borders to the sides, then sew the 4" x 37" borders to the top and bottom of the quilt.

2. Quilt as desired.

3. Bind with the 2 1/2" red strips.

Radiant Sapphire

104" x 104" | Embroidered block size: 14 7/8" x 14 7/8"
Pieced by Kaye Spitzli, embroidered by Kaye Spitzli and Arlene Lawson, quilted by Eula Lang. Pillow cases and sheet embroidered by Arlene Lawson.

Embroidery patterns for this quilt are on pages 83-86.

Quilts sometimes evolve over time rather than happening all at once. My mother-in-law made many beautiful quilts in her (too short) lifetime. The one that I particularly admired was her blue Broken Star quilt which she kept on her bed. I vowed that 'someday' I would make one too. Several years ago, I started the piecing, and was very happy with my colors. However, when the piecing was finished, I hit a road block. How should I finish the inset blocks? In vain, I tried to come up with an appliqué design. After a time that idea was dismissed and the plan changed to hand quilting with trapunto. Meanwhile, I saw my mom, Arlene Lawson, embroidering a quilt block with perle cotton. Immediately my dilemma was solved. This would be the perfect finish for my Broken Star. I am pleased with the end result and very happy that I did not rush the process.

The radiance of this quilt is created by the fabrics. Select fabrics in colors that blend, progressing from lightest to darkest. It is equally important that some of your fabric be prints to provide movement.

Fabric requirements/supplies
For the pieced star
- ♥ 1/4 yard Fabric 1 (lightest blue)
- ♥ 3/8 yard Fabric 2
- ♥ 5/8 yard Fabric 3
- ♥ 3/4 yard Fabric 4
- ♥ 7/8 yard Fabric 5 (medium blue)
- ♥ 1 1/8 yards Fabric 6
- ♥ 1 1/4 yards Fabric 7
- ♥ 1 1/8 yards Fabric 8

- ♥ 7/8 yard Fabric 9
- ♥ 3/4 yard Fabric 10 (dark blue)
- ♥ 5/8 yard Fabric 11
- ♥ 3/8 yard Fabric 12
- ♥ 1/4 yard Fabric 13 (darkest blue)

- ♥ 6 1/3 yards background fabric
- ♥ 1 3/4 yards outside border and binding
- ♥ 2 yards bleached muslin (to line the embroidery blocks)
- ♥ 9 skeins #5 DMC Perle Cotton 4230
- ♥ Embroidery needle size 7

Cutting instructions
13 star fabrics
From the 13 star fabrics, cut 2" x width of fabric strips in the following amounts:

- ♥ Fabric 1 - 3 strips
- ♥ Fabric 2 - 6 strips
- ♥ Fabric 3 - 9 strips
- ♥ Fabric 4 - 12 strips
- ♥ Fabric 5 - 15 strips
- ♥ Fabric 6 - 18 strips
- ♥ Fabric 7 - 21 strips
- ♥ Fabric 8 - 18 strips
- ♥ Fabric 9 - 15 strips
- ♥ Fabric 10 - 12 strips
- ♥ Fabric 11 - 9 strips
- ♥ Fabric 12 - 6 strips
- ♥ Fabric 13 - 3 strips

Background fabric

♥ Eight 18" squares

♥ Twelve 15 3/8" squares

♥ Two 22 1/4" squares cut in half diagonally twice to make 8 side setting triangles

Lining

♥ Eight 18" squares

Border and binding fabric

♥ Twelve 2" x width of fabric (wof) strips

♥ Twelve 2 1/2" x wof strips

Preparing embroidered inset blocks

1. Use a light box to trace the Daisy Bouquet pattern (from pages 83-84) onto each of the eight 18" blocks, centering the design on the block. Be careful with the placement so the floral pattern is on point.

2. Baste the lining fabric behind the traced pattern block. You may omit this step if your background fabric is a dark color.

3. Embroider all 8 blocks using the stem stitch with Perle Cotton #5. See pages 63-67 for embroidery instructions. Stitch through both layers of fabric. Press the blocks on the back side by placing them right side down on a soft surface to avoid crushing the stitching.

Assembling the quilt top

1. Join the 2" star fabric strips into sets, offsetting the beginning of each strip by 1 1/2" as shown. Press all the seam allowances in odd-numbered sets toward the top row and those in even-numbered sets toward the bottom row.

Strip set diagrams

Strip set 1 – make 3

Set One is shown above, make 3 of Set One. Make 3 of each of the following sets in this same manner.

Set Two: Fabric 2, Fabric 3, Fabric 4, Fabric 5, Fabric 6, Fabric 7, Fabric 8.

Set Three: Fabric 3, Fabric 4, Fabric 5, Fabric 6, Fabric 7, Fabric 8, Fabric 9.

Set Four: Fabric 4, Fabric 5, Fabric 6, Fabric 7, Fabric 8, Fabric 9, Fabric 10.

Set Five: Fabric 5, Fabric 6, Fabric 7, Fabric 8, Fabric 9, Fabric 10, Fabric 11.

Set Six: Fabric 6, Fabric 7, Fabric 8, Fabric 9, Fabric 10, Fabric 11, Fabric 12.

Set Seven: Fabric 7, Fabric 8, Fabric 9, Fabric 10, Fabric 11, Fabric 12, Fabric 13.

2. Place the 45° angle line of a 24" ruler along the outer straight edge (close to the end of a strip set) and cut a straight edge. Sub-cut the strip sets into 2" diamond strips. Cut 32 diamond strips from each of the 7 strip sets.

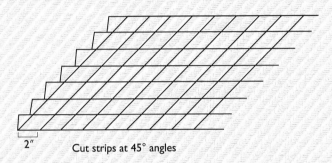

2"   Cut strips at 45° angles

3. Stitch one of each strip set together as shown to form the pieced diamond.

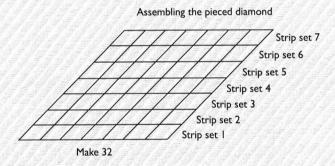

Assembling the pieced diamond

Strip set 7
Strip set 6
Strip set 5
Strip set 4
Strip set 3
Strip set 2
Strip set 1

Make 32

Make 32 pieced diamonds.

4. Join 2 pieced diamonds, matching colors and seam lines. Sew from the center out, beginning and ending each seam 1/4" from the edge with a backstitch. Make 4 units of 2 pieced diamonds.

5. Join 2 quarters to form the half star sewing from the center out. Join the 2 halves in the same manner.

6. Trim the embroidered blocks to 15 3/8" square, being careful to keep the embroidery centered.

7. To set an embroidered square in each corner of the star, place one side of the embroidered square to the arm of the star, right sides together. Stitch from the inside seam line to the outside edge. Align the remaining side with the arm of the opposite diamond and stitch from the inside seam line to the outside edge. Repeat this process with the remaining 7 embroidered squares.

8. Join the remaining pieced diamonds into 8 groups of 3 as shown. Set the diamond units to the embroidered squares in the same manner as in step 7.

9. Sew 2 side setting triangles into each of the 4 sides of the star in the same manner as the set-in squares in step 7.

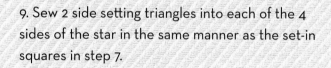

10. Join the 15 3/8" background squares into groups of 3 to form corner squares. Set the squares into the corners.

Borders/finishing

1. For the border, sew the 2" strips together. Measure the quilt at the left side, through the center, and the right side. Using the average measurement, cut 2 border strips this measurement and stitch to each side of the quilt.

2. Measure the quilt at the top, through the center, and at the bottom. Using the average measurement, cut the remaining 2 border strips this measurement and stitch to the top and bottom of the quilt.

3. Quilt as desired.

4. Bind with the 2 1/2" strips.

Kaye used the designs on pages 85-86 to embroider matching pillowcases and sheets.

Flit and Flutter

Queen size quilt 87" x 87"
Embroidered block size: 9" x 9"
Pieced and embroidered by Christina DeArmond, quilted by Eula Lang

Embroidery patterns for this quilt are on pages 87-88.

In this large version of Flit and Flutter, I used the curved appliquéd corners on the butterfly blocks. I like the graceful curve this method creates, however for a quicker finish you may use the snowball corner option. This is one of my favorite quilts: it is not difficult but has a simple elegance.

This quilt consists of 49 blocks, seven blocks wide by seven blocks deep, alternating the honey bee and butterfly blocks. There are 25 pieced honey bee blocks and 24 embroidered butterfly blocks.

The corners of the butterfly blocks may be appliquéd with a curve as shown in the photo or pieced using the snowball corner method. Instructions are included for both options.

Fabric requirements/supplies

- ♥ 5 yards background
- ♥ 2 yards total of assorted prints for piecing and appliqué
- ♥ 2 3/4 yards for border
- ♥ 3/4 yard for binding
- ♥ Embroidery floss in colors that complement your fabrics
- ♥ Embroidery needle size 7
- ♥ Fabric marking pencil or pen

Cutting instructions

From the background fabric cut:

- ♥ Twenty-four 10" blocks
- ♥ One hundred 2 3/4" squares for honey bee blocks
- ♥ One hundred 2 3/4" x 5" rectangles for honey bee blocks
- ♥ One hundred 2" squares
- ♥ Four strips 5" x 66 1/2" for the butterfly embroidered border
- ♥ Four 5" squares for the butterfly border corners

From the assorted prints cut:

Corner options for butterfly blocks—choose ONE of these options, NOT both.

Option 1 - appliqué corners:

- ♥ Make a freezer paper template (see page 88, add 1/4" seam allowance on all sides as you cut). From the assorted prints, cut 4 matching corners for each of the 24 blocks (96 corners).

or

Option 2 - snowball corners:

- ♥ From the assorted prints, cut 4 matching 3 1/2" squares for each of the 24 blocks (96 corners).

For the Honey Bee blocks:

- ♥ 25 sets of five 2" squares cut from the same fabric (125 squares total)
- ♥ 25 sets of bee bodies and wings (one set is 4 bodies and 8 wings): a total of 100 bodies and 200 wings

From the border fabric cut:

The fabric requirement includes sufficient fabric to cut the inner and outer borders from the length of the fabric.***Do not cut the fabric crosswise.**

- ♥ Two 2"x 63 1/2" strips for inner border
- ♥ Two 2" x 66 1/2" strips for inner border
- ♥ Two 6 1/2" x 75 1/2" strips for outer border
- ♥ Two 6 1/2" x 87 1/2" strips for outer border

From the binding fabric cut:

- ♥ Ten 2 1/2" by the width of the fabric (wof) strips

Butterfly blocks

1. Trace the large butterfly (see page 88), centering it on each of the 24 - 10" squares using a fabric marking pencil or pen.

2. Embroider with a stem stitch on the traced lines using 2 strands of embroidery floss. Press the blocks from the back.

3. Trim the blocks to 9 1/2" square, keeping the embroidery centered.

Option 1 - butterfly block corners—appliqué method

1. Using the freezer paper template of the appliqué corner pattern (see page 88) pressed on the right side of the desired fabric, mark the curve. Cut out.

2. Glue baste each corner in place, then hand appliqué the curves.

Option 1

Option 2 - butterfly block corners—snowball method:

Instead of steps 1 and 2 above, follow these steps:

1. Draw a diagonal line across the center of each of the 3 1/2" squares.

2. With right sides together, place one square in EACH corner of the 9 1/2" background squares.

3. Stitch on this line, trim away the corner point and press the resulting triangle back to form the 9 1/2" square blocks.

Option 2

Butterfly border

1. On the four 5" x 66 1/2" background border strips, measure in the 1/4" seam allowance on each end and then divide the border into 6 equal 11" segments.

2. Mark these divisions with a pencil (within the seam allowance) or by using pins.

3. Trace the 11" border pattern piece (see page 87) that contains 2 small butterflies and swirls, centering this pattern within the 11" segments of border fabric. Repeat for the length of the piece and for the other 3 sides.

4. Embroider the border with 2 strands of floss, choosing colors that were used in the other butterfly blocks. We used yellow floss for all the swirls.

Butterfly border corners

1. Trace one butterfly on point from the border pattern piece onto each of the four 5" background border blocks for the 4 corners.

2. Embroider these 4 corner blocks with 2 strands of floss.

Honey Bee blocks

1. Make nine patch blocks using the 2" squares, with 5 print and 4 background pieces in each nine patch. Use a matching set of 5 print squares in each block.

C=color

2. Attach a background 2 3/4" x 5" rectangle to the top and bottom of each nine patch. Press toward the rectangle.

3. Make side units by sewing a 2 3/4" square on each end of the 2 3/4" x 5" rectangles. Press toward the centers.

All parts are light

4. Attach a side unit to the 2 sides of the nine patch unit.

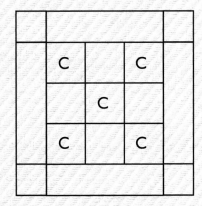

5. Honey Bee body parts can be appliquéd either by hand or fused on and then stitched around.

♥ For hand appliqué, make a freezer paper template of the Large Bee Wing and the Large Bee Body patterns. Press the templates onto the right sides of the desired fabrics, mark with a marking pencil, and cut out leaving a 1/4" seam allowance. Glue baste in place, referring to the photo for placement, then hand appliqué.

♥ For fusible appliqué, blanket stitch around the shapes after they are fused onto the block.

Make 25 honey bee blocks.

Assembling the quilt

1. Arrange the butterfly and honey bee blocks in a pleasing color order alternating the butterflies and honey bees. Start with a honey bee block in the first row and end with a honey bee block. Row 1 will have 7 blocks (4 honey bee, 3 butterfly).

2. Row 2 will start and end with a butterfly block.

3. Make a total of 7 rows each having 7 blocks across. Make 4 of Row 1 and 3 of Row 2.

4. Assemble the rows alternating Rows 1 and 2, beginning and ending with Row 1.

5. Sew the 2" x 63 1/2" inner border strips to the sides of the quilt.

6. Sew the 2" x 66 1/2" inner border strips to the top and bottom of the quilt.

7. Sew a 5" x 66 1/2" butterfly border strip to both sides of the quilt.

8. Piece a 5" corner butterfly square on each end of the other 2 butterfly border strips, being careful which direction the butterflies are facing. (We have them facing toward the outer corner.)

9. Sew these 2 butterfly borders to the top and bottom of the quilt.

10. Sew the 6 1/2" x 75 1/2" outer border strips to the sides of the quilt.

11. Sew the 6 1/2" x 87 1/2" outer border strips to the top and bottom of the quilt.

12. Quilt as desired.

13. Piece together the binding strips and apply to the quilt.

Flit and Flutter Baby Quilt

42" x 54"
Embroidered block size: 6" x 6"
Pieced, embroidered, and quilted by Christina DeArmond

Embroidery patterns for this quilt are on page 87.

Your favorite little angel will love cuddling this cute quilt. I used the snowball corner option when making this size. I used 1930s reproduction fabrics in pastels, but it would be just as cute in bright colors.

Fabric requirements/supplies

- ♥ 1 2/3 yards background
- ♥ 3/4 yard total assorted prints for piecing and appliqué
- ♥ 1/2 yard inner border
- ♥ 3/4 yard outer border
- ♥ 1/2 yard binding
- ♥ Embroidery floss in colors that complement your fabrics
- ♥ Embroidery needle size 7

Cutting instructions

From the background fabric cut:
- ♥ Seventeen 7" squares for butterflies
- ♥ Seventy-two 2" squares for honey bee blocks
- ♥ Seventy-two 2" x 3 1/2" rectangles for honey bee blocks
- ♥ Seventy-two 1 1/2" squares for nine patch centers of honey bee blocks

From the assorted print fabrics cut:
- ♥ 17 sets of four 2 1/2" squares (68 squares total), one set for the snowball corners of each of the butterfly blocks.

- ♥ 18 sets of five 1 1/2" squares (90 squares total), one set for each of the honey bee blocks

- ♥ 18 sets of bee bodies and wings (one set is 4 bodies and 8 wings) - a total of 72 bodies and 144 wings

From the inner border fabric cut:
- ♥ Two 2 1/2" x 42 1/2" strips
- ♥ Two 2 1/2" x 34 1/2" strips

From the outer border fabric cut:
- ♥ Five 4 1/2" x width of fabric strips. Cut and piece these strips to make 2 border strips that measure 4 1/2" x 46 1/2" for the sides and 2 pieces that measure 4 1/2" x 42 1/2" for the top and bottom.

From the binding fabric cut:
- ♥ Five strips 2 1/2" x width of fabric and piece together.

Butterfly blocks

Make 17 butterfly blocks following the directions for the queen sized quilt on page 32 with these changes:

1. Trace the small butterfly pattern onto the 7" background squares.

2. Trim the blocks to 6 1/2" square after the embroidery is completed.

3. Use the snowball corner method and the 2 1/2" squares of the assorted fabrics to make the butterfly blocks.

Honey bee blocks

Make 18 honey bee blocks following the directions for the queen sized quilt on page 30 with these changes:

1. Make nine patch block centers using the 1 1/2" squares.

2. Surround the nine patch blocks using the 2" squares and 2" x 3 1/2" rectangles.

3. Appliqué the small honey bee body and wings in place.

Assembling the quilt

1. Place the butterfly and honey bee blocks in a pleasing order, alternating the butterflies and honey bees. Start with a honey bee block in the first row and end with a honey bee block. Row 1 will have 5 blocks (3 honey bee, 2 butterfly). Make 4. Row 2 will start and end with a butterfly block. Make 3. Stitch the rows together: Row 1, then Row 2; repeat; end with Row 1.

2. Sew the 2" x 42 1/2" inner border strips to the sides of the quilt.

3. Sew the 2" x 34 1/2" inner border strips to the top and bottom of the quilt.

4. Sew a 4 1/2" x 46 1/2" outer border strip to both sides of the quilt.

5. Sew the 4 1/2" x 42 1/2" outer border strips to the top and bottom of the quilt.

6. Quilt as desired.

7. Piece together the binding strips and apply to the quilt.

Flit and Flutter Tabletopper

35" x 35"
Embroidered block size: 9" x 9"
Pieced and embroidered by Christina DeArmond

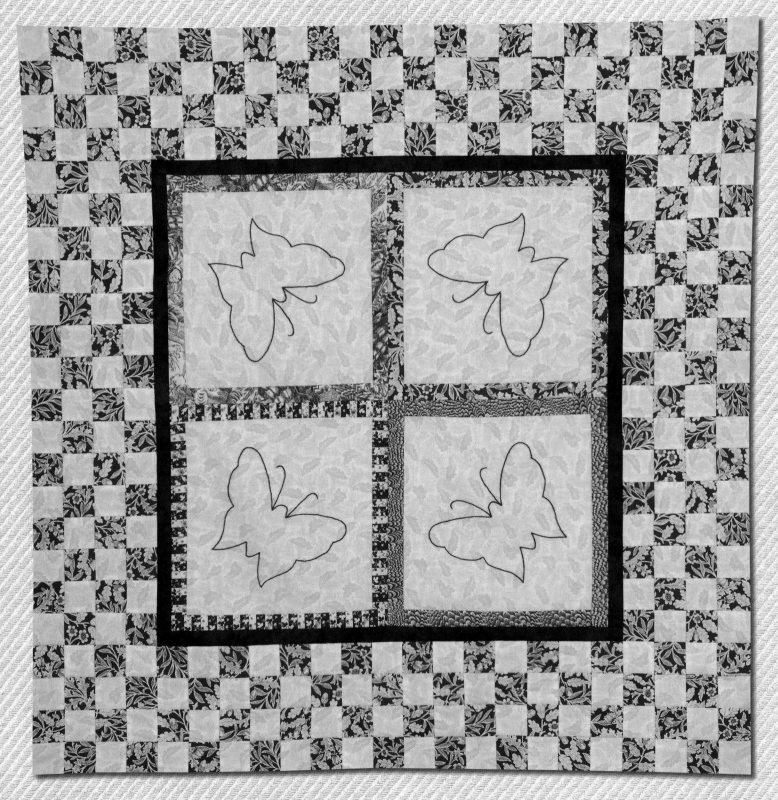

Embroidery patterns for this quilt are on page 88.

Ijust had to try out these butterflies in traditional redwork. They make a cute table topper and can be finished quickly.

Fabric requirements
- ♥ 1/3 yard background
- ♥ 1/8 yard each of 4 fabrics for sashing
- ♥ 1/4 yard for inner border
- ♥ 3/4 each of 2 fabrics for outer checkerboard border
- ♥ 1/3 yard binding
- ♥ Embroidery floss in colors that complement your fabrics
- ♥ Embroidery needle size 7

Cutting instructions
From the background fabric cut:
- ♥ Four 10" squares for embroidered butterflies

From the 4 sashing fabrics cut:
- ♥ Two 1 1/4" x 9 1/2" rectangles from each of the 4 pieces (8 total)
- ♥ Two 1 1/4" x 11" rectangles from each of the 4 pieces (8 total)

From the inner border fabric cut:
- ♥ Two 1 1/4" x 21 1/2" strips
- ♥ Two 1 1/4" x 23" strips

From the 2 checkerboard fabrics cut:
- ♥ Eight 2" strips x wof from each (16 strips total)

From the binding fabric cut:
- ♥ Four 2 1/2" x width of fabric strips

Embroidery instructions
1. Trace one large butterfly **on point** on each of the four 10" squares.

2. Embroider with stem stitch using 2 strands of embroidery floss.

3. Trim blocks to 9 1/2".

Piecing instructions
1. Sew 2 matching 1 1/4" x 9 1/2" strips to top and bottom of a butterfly block. Press seams toward sashing.

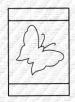

2. Sew the matching 1 1/4" x 11" strips to the sides of the butterfly block. Press seams toward sashing.

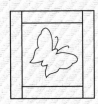

3. Continue doing steps one and two for the remaining 3 butterfly blocks.

4. Sew the sashed butterfly blocks together to make a four patch.

5. Sew one 1 1/4" x 21 1/2" inner border strip to both

sides of the four patch butterfly unit.

6. Sew one 1 1/4" x 23" inner border strip to top and bottom of the four patch butterfly unit.

Assembly of checkerboard blocks

1. Make a strip set by sewing 2 of each of the checkerboard fabrics together alternating fabrics—1, 2, 1, 2.

2. Press toward the darker color strips. The pressing is very important as this will allow for the seams to fit closely up to each other and make crisp points.

3. Make 3 more of the above strip sets: make a total of 4.

4. Cut each of the strips sets every 2" to make a total of 68 strip units that measure 2" x 6 1/2".

5. Piece the sets together turning every other one so that a checkerboard effect is achieved.

6. Make 2 sets with 15 strips units in each set.

7. Make 2 sets with 19 strips units in each set.

8. Sew one of the 15 strip sets to the opposite sides of the butterfly four patch.

9. Sew one of the 19 strip sets to the top and one to the bottom of the butterfly four patch.

10. Quilt as desired.

11. Piece together the binding strips and apply to the quilt.

Flit and Flutter wallhanging
Pieced and embroidered by Christina
DeArmond, quilted by Eula Lang

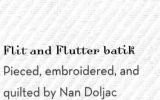

Flit and Flutter batik
Pieced, embroidered, and
quilted by Nan Doljac

Stitches of Wisdom

50" x 71"

Embroidered block size: 8 1/2" x 10 1/2"

Pieced and embroidered by Arlene Lawson, quilted by Eula Lang

Embroidery patterns for this quilt are on pages 89-100.

Stitches of Wisdom is a quilt that is filled with verses from the Bible's Book of Proverbs. We chose 12 of our favorite proverbs and designed embroidery blocks to depict them. Part of each verse is embroidered in the block, while the whole verse is included in the instructions. There is simple piecing around each block to enhance it. You can make the setting fabrics blend together or they can have a lot of contrast as in the redwork quilt.

Fabric requirements/supplies

- ♥ 1 1/2 yards neutral fabric for embroidery background
- ♥ 2/3 yard sashing and inner border
- ♥ 1 1/4 yards outer border
- ♥ 1/2 yard binding
- ♥ Permanent marker: pigma pen or jelly roll pen
- ♥ Floss (your favorite red)
- ♥ Embroidery needle size 7

The pieced frames surrounding each embroidered block require 2 fabrics per block, the main fabric (rectangles and triangles) and the accent fabric (triangles). We include several options for selecting these fabrics.

If you make all the blocks from the same 2 fabrics, you need:

- ♥ 1 1/4 yards main fabric
- ♥ 2/3 yard accent fabric

If you make 6 blocks each of 2 different color combinations, you need:

- ♥ 3/4 yard each of 2 main fabrics
- ♥ 3/8 yard each of 2 accent fabrics

If you make 4 blocks each of 3 different color combinations, you need:

- ♥ 1/2 yard each of 3 main fabrics
- ♥ 1/4 yard each of 3 accent fabrics

If you make 3 blocks each of 4 different color combinations, you need:

- ♥ 1/2 yard each of 4 main fabrics
- ♥ 1/4 yard each of 4 accent fabrics

If you make 2 blocks each of 6 different color combinations, you need:

- ♥ 3/8 yard each of 6 main fabrics
- ♥ 1/8 yard each of 6 accent fabrics

Cutting instructions
Blocks:

- ♥ Piece A: Cut 12 neutral background rectangles 10" x 14" for the embroidery. These will be trimmed to 8 1/2" x 10 1/2" after they are embroidered.

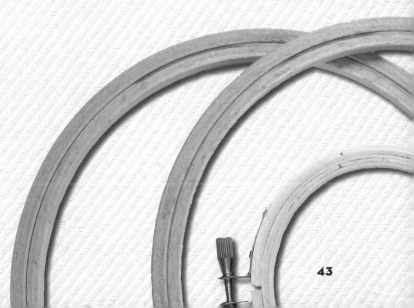

Pieced block frames—for EACH of 12 blocks cut (refer to the block diagram on page 48):

- ♥ Two 2 1/2" x 6 1/2" rectangles for piece B (main fabric)

- ♥ Two 2 1/2" x 4 1/2" rectangles for piece C (main fabric)

- ♥ Six 2 7/8" squares cut in half diagonally once for piece D (main fabric)

- ♥ Six 2 7/8" squares cut in half diagonally once for piece E (accent fabric)

Sashing and inner border:

- ♥ Eight 1 1/2" x 14 1/2" rectangles for vertical sashing strips

- ♥ Nine 1 1/2" x 12 1/2" rectangles for horizontal sashing strips

- ♥ Five 1 1/2" x width of fabric (wof) strips for inner border

- ♥ Six 1 1/2" squares for cornerstones

Outer border:

- ♥ Six 5 1/2" x wof strips pieced together and cut into:

  - ❖ Two 5 1/2" x 50 1/2" strips for top and bottom borders

  - ❖ Two 5 1/2" x 61 1/2" strips for side borders

Binding:

- ♥ Six 2 1/2" x wof strips

Embroidery Instructions

The blocks in this quilt were each designed to represent the message in a Bible verse from the Book of Proverbs. We've included the original verse with the block instructions.

Trace each picture onto one of the 10" x 14" pieces of neutral fabric using a permanent marker, being careful to center the design on the block. For more about the stitches, refer to the embroidery instructions on pages 63-67.

Pleasant Words block

Proverbs 16:24: "Pleasant words are as a honeycomb, sweet to the soul, and health to the bones."

1. Using 2 strands of floss, stem stitch the flower, stem, leaves, bee, and honeycomb.

2. Using 2 strands of floss, back stitch the words.

3. Using one strand of floss, stem stitch the details in the bee's wings, the veins in the leaves, the bee's antenna, and the detail in the top of the coneflower.

Sunrise on the Beach block

Proverbs 4:18: "But the path of the just is as the shining light, that shineth more and more unto the perfect day."

1. Using 2 strands of floss, stem stitch the sun, the horizon, the sun rays, and the ocean waves.

2. Using 2 stands of floss, backstitch the words.

3. Using one strand of floss, back stitch the foot prints, the outside of the sand dollar, and the shell.

4. Using one strand of floss, make 5 lazy daisy stitches to fill in the middle of the sand dollar.

Basket of Apples block

Proverbs 7:2: "Keep my commandments, and live; and my law as the apple of thine eye."

1. Using 2 strands of floss, stem stitch the outside of the basket, the band of the basket, the apples, and the handles on the basket.

2. Using 2 strands of floss, backstitch the words.

3. Using one strand of floss, stem stitch the leaves, the apple stem, and the grass.

Bible and Candle block

Proverbs 4:5: "Get wisdom, get understanding: forget it not; neither decline from the words of my mouth."

1. Using 2 strands of floss, stem stitch the Bible, the Bible pages, the ribbon, the candle stand, the candle, and the flame.

2. Using 2 strands of floss, back stitch the words.

3. Using one strand of floss, stem stitch the rays coming from the candle glow.

4. Using one strand of floss, back stitch the melting wax.

Heart block

Proverbs 17.22: "A merry heart doeth good like a medicine: but a broken spirit drieth the bones."

1. Using 2 strands of floss, stem stitch the heart.

2. Using 2 strands of floss, backstitch the words.

3. Using one strand of floss, backstitch the small circles that border the inside of the heart.

Covered Bridge block

Proverbs 4:27: "Turn not to the right hand nor to the left: remove thy foot from evil."

1. Using 2 strands of floss, stem stitch the outside line of the bridge, the river both behind the bridge and in front of the bridge, the pillars, and the ground leading up to the bridge.

2. Using 2 stands of floss, backstitch the words.

3. Using one strand of floss, stem stitch the line details on the bridge, the bridge railing, posts for railing, and the water swirls.

4. Using one strand of floss, backstitch the stones.

Well block

Proverbs 5:15: "Drink waters out of thine own cistern, and running waters out of thine own well."

1. Using 2 strands of floss, stem stitch the well roof, the pole that holds the bucket, and the bucket.

2. Using 2 strands of floss, back stitch the words.

3. Using one strand of floss, stem stitch the bucket handle, the rope, roof details, and the grass.

4. Using one strand of floss, back stitch the stones and the wood detail on the post.

5. Using one strand of floss, use a stem stitch to make the rope that is wound around the pole.

A Garland of Grace block

Proverbs 4:9: "She shall give to thine head an ornament of grace: a crown of glory shall she deliver to thee."

1. Using 2 strands of floss, stem stitch the oval frame, the leaves, the stems.

2. Using 2 stands of floss, backstitch the words.

3. Using 2 strands of floss, make lazy daisies for the flower petals.

4. Using one strand of floss, stem stitch the leaf details.

Tower block

Proverbs 18:10: "The name of the LORD is a strong tower: the righteous runneth into it, and is safe."

1. Using 2 strands of floss, stem stitch the castle, flag pole, flag, and the clouds.

2. Using 2 strands of floss, back stitch the words.

3. Using one strand of floss, stem stitch the castle details.

4. Using two strands of floss, satin stitch the top of the pole.

Harvest block

Proverbs 3:9: "Honor the LORD with thy substance, and with the first fruits of all thine increase:"

1. Using 2 strands of floss, stem stitch the pumpkin, wheat stalks, and the leaf.

2. Using 2 strands of floss, backstitch the grapes and the words.

3. Using one strand of floss, stem stitch the grass, the lines in between the wheat stalks, and the veins in the leaf.

4. Using one stand of floss, use a stem stitch to make the wheat details.

Clock block

Proverbs 3:2: "For length of days, and long life, and peace, shall they add to thee."

1. Using 2 strands of floss, stem stitch the clock, the clock stand, and the pendulum.

2. Using 2 strands of floss, back stitch the words.

3. Using one strand of floss, stem stitch the hands of the clock.

4. Using one strand of floss, using a stem stitch to make the time markings.

Clothesline block

Proverbs 31:30: "Favor is deceitful, and beauty is vain: but a woman that fears the LORD, she shall be praised."

1. Using 2 strands of floss, stem stitch the clothes line posts, the clothesline, the outside of the quilt, and the laundry basket.

2. Using 2 strands of floss, backstitch the words.

3. Using one strand of floss, stem stitch the post

details, the lines inside the quilt, the grass, and the basket details.

4. Using one strand of floss, backstitch the clothes in the laundry basket.

**NOTE: Before piecing the blocks, arrange the embroidery blocks in a pleasing manner and decide how the block frame color combinations should be arranged.

Block piecing instructions

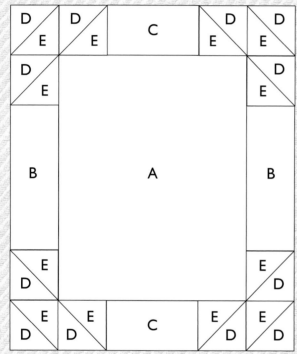

Block diagram

1. Trim all of the embroidery blocks to 8 1/2" x 10 1/2", keeping the embroidery centered on the block.

2. Place triangles D and E right sides together and stitch along the long side to make squares.

3. Sew one D/E square to each end of piece B, making sure the accent triangles (E) are facing the right direction. Repeat to make 2 units.

4. Sew one unit to each side of the block.

5. With 4 D/E squares, sew 2 squares to each end of piece C. Repeat to make 2 units.

6. Sew one to the top and one to the bottom of the block.

7. Repeat this process with the other eleven blocks.

Quilt assembly

1. Sew 4 rows. Each consists of a block, a 1 1/2" x 14 1/2" sashing strip, a block, a 1 1/2" x 14 1/2" sashing strip, a block.

2. Make 3 strips of horizontal sashing by sewing together a 1 1/2" x 12 1/2" strip, a cornerstone, a 1 1/2" x 12 1/2" strip, a cornerstone, a 1 1/2" x 12 1/2" strip.

3. Sew the top together by sewing: a row, a horizontal sashing strip, a row, a horizontal sashing strip, a row, a sashing strip, a row.

4. Sew a 1 1/2" x 59 1/2" inner border to each side of the quilt.

5. Sew a 1 1/2" x 40 1/2" inner border to the top and bottom of the quilt.

6. Sew a 5 1/2" x 61 1/2" outer border strip to each side of the quilt.

7. Sew a 5 1/2" x 50 1/2" outer border strip to the top and bottom of the quilt.

8. Layer and quilt as desired.

9. Bind.

Stitches of Wisdom with silk floss
Pieced and embroidered by Christina DeArmond, quilted by Eula Lang

Vintage Daisies

Quilt size: 37 1/2" x 37 1/2"
Embroidered block size: 15" x 15"
Pieced by Christina DeArmond, Eula Lang, Nan Doljac, Kaye Spitzli; embroidered
by Christina DeArmond, Eula Lang, Nan Doljac; quilted by Christina DeArmond

Embroidery patterns for this quilt are on pages 101–105.

Vintage Daisies was made in a round robin fashion. I have always loved daisies so my starting block was the embroidered daisies with the flag in the middle. The quilt has an old-fashioned look, so I used a lot of browns and pinks. After the center was finished, the block was passed to Eula who added the wallpaper stripe scalloped border and she filled in the center embroidery with a few more leaves. The quilt was then passed on to Kaye, who made the Churn Dash border. Nan Doljac added the final embroidered scalloped border.

Fabric requirements/supplies

- ♥ 2 yards cream background
- ♥ Fat quarter striped wallpaper print
- ♥ 1/4 yard pink accent
- ♥ 3/8 yard brown print
- ♥ 7/8 yard brown/pink floral outer border/binding
- ♥ Embroidery floss-1 skein each of several pinks and greens, a brown and a yellow
- ♥ Brown Pigma pen
- ♥ Light box
- ♥ Embroidery needle size 7

Cutting instructions

From the cream background fabric:
- ♥ One 16" square
- ♥ Twenty-four 2 1/8" squares cut in half diagonally once: 48 half-square triangles (hst)
- ♥ Two 1 1/8" x width of fabric (wof) strips
- ♥ Twelve 1 3/4" squares
- ♥ Eight 3 5/8" squares cut in half diagonally once (16 corner setting triangles-cst)
- ♥ Four 6 5/8" squares cut in half diagonally twice (16 side setting triangles-sst)
- ♥ Four 5 3/4" squares
- ♥ Four 5 1/2" by wof strips

From the wallpaper fabric:
- ♥ One 15 1/2" square

From the pink accent fabric:
- ♥ Two 1" x 15 1/2" strips
- ♥ Two 1" x 16 1/2" strips
- ♥ Two 1" x 28" strips
- ♥ Two 1" x 29" strips

From the brown print fabric:
- ♥ Twenty-four 2 1/8" squares cut in half diagonally once (48 hst)
- ♥ Two 1 1/8" x wof strips

From the brown/pink floral outer border/binding fabric:
- ♥ Four 4" x wof strips
- ♥ Four 2 1/2" x wof strips

Assembly instructions
Center embroidery:

1. Using a light box and Pigma pen, center and then trace the basket of flowers block onto the 16" square of background fabric.

2. Embroider your block using color(s) that co-ordinate with your print fabrics.

3. Press the block from the back then trim it to 15 1/2" square, being careful to keep the embroidery centered.

Matting (wallpaper):

1. Take a 15 1/2" square of freezer paper. Fold it in half from top to bottom and again from side to side forming a four layered, folded square.

2. Using the pattern provided on page 103, trace the inside cutting line of the center block matting, being careful to align cut edges of folded paper and the marked "cut edges" of the pattern.

3. Cut out the freezer paper pattern on the traced line.

4. Unfold the freezer paper and iron it to the right side of a 15 1/2" square of matting (wallpaper) fabric.

5. Draw a line on the fabric along the curved edge of the freezer paper. This is your guide line for turning under when appliquéing.

6. Remove the freezer paper and trim away the center of the matting fabric a scant 1/4" inside the drawn line.

7. Layer the embroidery block right side up, then the matting fabric, right side up. Baste the two pieces together.

8. Appliqué the matting to the embroidery block, turning under the seam allowance and the guideline as you go.

9. Stem stitch (embroider) an accent line just next to the matting edge all the way around the center block.

10. Sew a 1" x 15 1/2" strip of accent fabric to each side of the block. Press the seams toward the accent strips.

11. Sew a 1" x 16 1/2" strip of accent fabric to the top and one to the bottom edge of the block. Press the seams toward the accent strips.

Churn Dash Border
To make 12 Churn Dash blocks:

1. Sew one cream hst to one brown hst, press the seam toward the darker fabric. Repeat until you have 48 cream/brown half square triangle units for the corner squares of the churn dash blocks.

2. Sew one 1 1/8" cream strip to one 1 1/8" brown strip. Press the seam toward the brown. Repeat with the other strips. Cut forty-eight 1 3/4" sections for the side sections of the churn dash blocks.

3. Sew a side section to each side of a 1 3/4" cream square. Note color placement. Repeat to make 12 center units.

C = cream
B = brown

4. Sew a hst unit to each side of a side section. Note color placement. Repeat to make 24 outer units.

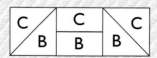

5. Sew an outer unit to the top and the bottom of a center unit. Repeat to make 12 Churn Dash blocks.

Setting triangles for Churn Dash border:

1. Sew a corner setting triangles (cst) to each of 2 sides of 8 of the churn dash blocks.

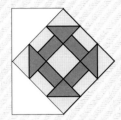

2. Using the sst and Churn Dash units, assemble 4 side strips as shown below.

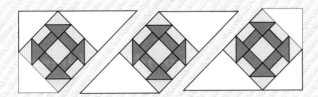

3. Sew one strip to each side of the quilt. Press.

Corner blocks

1. Trace and embroider the corner daisy motif on all four 5 3/4" cream squares.

2. Sew one square to each end of the 2 remaining churn dash strips.

3. Sew these to the top and bottom of the quilt.

Accent border

1. Sew a 1" x 28" pink accent strip to each side of the quilt. Press.

2. Sew a 1" x 29" strip to the top edge and one to the bottom edge of the quilt. Press.

Outer border/finishing

1. Sew one cream 5 1/2" by width of fabric strip to each of the 4 sides of the quilt matching the center of each strip to the center of each side. The strips will extend beyond the corners.

2. Miter the corners.

3. Using the pattern provided, cut a freezer paper template for the outer frame. Press this onto the right side of the 4" brown/pink floral strips. Draw a line along the curved edge of the freezer paper. Remove the freezer paper.

4. Trim the fabric a scant 1/4" from the curved line.

5. Appliqué these brown/pink floral pieces onto the outer edge of the cream border.

6. Trace the border embroidery pattern onto the cream section of the outer border.

7. Embroider the outer border.

8. Quilt as desired.

9. Cut four 2 1/2" strips of binding fabric. Join them together and bind your quilt.

Abbreviations

corner setting triangles=cst

half-square triangles=hst

side setting triangles=sst

width of fabric=wof

Projects

Welcome

8" x 16"
By Christina DeArmond

At a quilt show, I watched a woman demonstrate twilling. I was fascinated, watching how the knots all looked so perfect. She gave me a lesson and I was hooked. I really enjoy twilling. It is fun to do and your project will be completed before you know it.

The embroidery pattern for this project is on pages 106-107.

Material requirements

- ♥ Cream fabric - 1/2 yard
- ♥ Aunt Lydia crochet thread size 10
- ♥ Large crewel needle
- ♥ Fabric stabilizer (fusible) - 1/2 yard
- ♥ Brown Pigma pen 01
- ♥ Embroidery hoop
- ♥ 8" x 16" purchased picture frame with mounting board

Instructions

- ♥ Iron the stabilizer onto the back of the cream fabric, following the manufacturer's instructions.
- ♥ Trace the Welcome design onto the fabric using the brown Pigma pen.
- ♥ Place the fabric in the embroidery hoop. Using a large crewel needle and 2 strands of thread, make rows of knots (twilling—see instructions on page 67) along each traced line of each letter to form "Welcome" according to the diagram on pages 106-107.
- ♥ Using 2 strands of thread, make French knots on the dots that surround WELCOME.
- ♥ Stretch the finished design over a mounting board and place in the frame.

Bread Basket Liner

By Christina DeArmond

Kaye has a treasured wedding gift, a pair of embroidered pillowcases in white on white. All she knew was that the stitching was called "German Knot". When Christy learned to twill, we were reintroduced to that stitch. It adds an elegant touch to a Bread cloth, or any other linens.

The embroidery pattern for this project is on page 108.

Material requirements

- ♥ Purchased bread cloth or napkin– approximately 18" square
- ♥ #5 weight Perle cotton
- ♥ Size #3 crewel embroidery needle
- ♥ Embroidery hoop
- ♥ Blue erasable marking pen

Instructions

1. Trace the design from page 108 onto the corner of the cloth using the erasable marking pen.

2. Using ONE strand of perle cotton, stitch the design using the twilling stitch (also known as the double knot stitch—see instructions on pages 63-67). Stitches will need to be close together (approx. 1/8"-1/4") as the script is fairly small.

3. When you finish the stitching, spray with water to remove the pen marks.

Place in basket, and enjoy!

Calendar Wallhanging

15 1/2" x 15 1/2"
Finished size embroidered block: 8" square
Stitched by Kaye Spitzli

The calendar blocks in the antique quilt inspired me to make individual calendar wall hangings. I plan to hang one in my home, changing it out each month. I am using a decorative hanger but a dowel rod, a yardstick cut to size or a decorative cafe rod would work as well. Just use your imagination! I thought variegated floss would be perfect for blending the colors in the flowers.

Embroidery patterns for this project are on pages 109-120.

Fabric requirements/supplies

Listed are the requirements to make ONE monthly wallhanging

- ♥ Fat quarter background fabric for the embroidery block
- ♥ Fat quarter muslin for lining the embroidery block
- ♥ 1/8 yard contrasting fabric for the border strip
- ♥ 3/4 yard print fabric for the border and bias binding
- ♥ Variegated embroidery floss to coordinate with your border fabric (see the tips on using variegated floss on page 61)
- ♥ Brown Pigma Pen
- ♥ Embroidery needle size 7

Cutting instructions

Background fabric:
- ♥ 12" square

Muslin:
- ♥ 12" square

Contrasting border strip:
- ♥ Four 1" x 8 1/2" strips

Borders:
- ♥ Two 5" x 8 1/2" strips
- ♥ Two 5" x 17 1/2" strips

Binding (after cutting the borders, from the remaining fabric cut):
- ♥ Five 2 1/2" bias strips cut at a 45° angle

Tabs for hanging
- ♥ Four 2" x 3" rectangles

Assembly

1. Trace the embroidery pattern, centering it on the 12" background fabric square. Baste the muslin to the back before stitching. Using the stem stitch, satin stitch, and French knots (refer to pages 63-67 for embroidery instructions), work the embroidered block. Press face down on a soft surface. Trim the block to 8 1/2" square, keeping the embroidery centered.

2. Take the four 1" x 8 1/2" contrast strips. Press each strip in half lengthwise, wrong sides together. Place a strip on one side of the embroidery block, raw edges together with the fold towards the center of the block. Baste the strip in place. Repeat on the opposite side then the top and the bottom. The strips will overlap at the corners.

3. Sew a 5" x 8 1/2" border fabric strip to each side of the block. Press. Sew 5" x 17 1/2" border fabric strips to the top and to the bottom of the block.

4. Mark the scalloped edge using the template on page 121. Quilt as desired. Trim on the marked scallop line.

5. Fold the hanging tab rectangles in half lengthwise right sides together and stitch. Turn right sides out. Pin one to each of the four highest points at the back of the top border. Bind using the 2 1/2" bias strips, catching the tabs in the seam as you sew. Sew down the binding. Turn under 1/4" on the end of each tab and whip stitch in place.

Tips for using variegated floss

The position of your cut on the variegated floss will determine the placement of color in your embroidery. The end of the floss that you knot will become the first stitches. In smaller areas of a pattern—a petal or leaf for instance—you may want to begin or end at specific shades of the color range, or not use a section at all (if it is too light or dark for that area or blends into the background). Study the range of shading and cut a working length for the section you will begin stitching first.

Think ahead. When using one skein of variegated floss over a large portion of the pattern, pull out a complete length of the color range. Within this color range, select the shade of floss which has the longest length. Cut a section of floss from the middle of this length to the middle of the next section of the same shade. Then depending on the length of these sections, cut them into working lengths for stitching. Use these lengths in the order cut so the color will blend from lightest to darkest rather than jump from light to dark.

Embroidery Instructions

Follow the instructions below to make the embroidery stitches we used on our quilts.

When using light colored fabric and darker thread, we recommend backing your block with muslin or interfacing to keep the knots and threads from showing through to the right side of the fabric. Stitch through both layers as though they are one. Place your block in an embroidery hoop with the fabric pulled taut, but not drum tight.

For the stem stitch, French knot and satin stitch, we used a size 7 embroidery needle threaded with one strand of 16 weight perle cotton OR two strands of embroidery floss. The floss is not doubled.

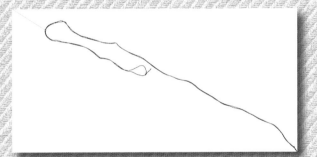

Knotting your thread

1. Knot the end of your floss by placing the floss across your index finger.

2. Place the needle on top of the floss.

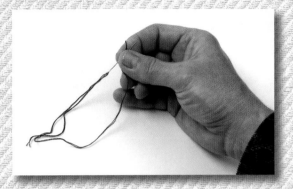

3. Wrap the long end of the floss around the needle twice.

4. Pinch the needle and thread wraps between your thumb and index finger.

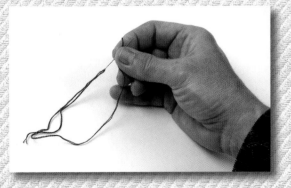

5. Pull the needle through to form the knot.

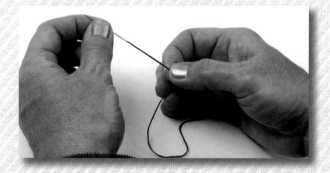

Stem Stitch

1. Insert the needle from the back, coming up on the top/right side at the beginning of the line you wish to embroider.

2. Insert the needle back into the stitching line about 1/8" from the starting point. Travel across the back side of the line, with the tip coming back to the top of the fabric half way between these two points. Pull the needle through until the thread is smooth and flat against the fabric, being careful not to pull so tight that you cause the fabric to pucker. This is one stitch.

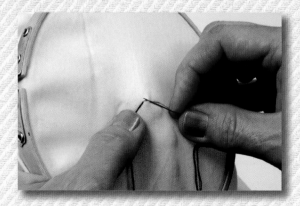

3. Insert the needle back into the stitching line about 1/8" from the point you just came out of. Travel across the back side of the line with the tip coming back to the top of the fabric just to the right of the end of the first stitch. Pull the needle through to form the second stitch. Continue this process the full length of each line.

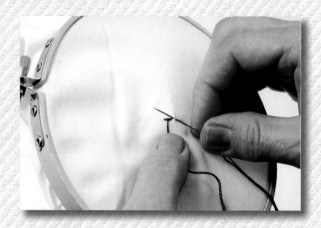

4. To tie off a thread, insert the needle through the fabric to the back side and pull the thread through. Weave the needle back and forth between the stitches you have just made, pull the thread through and cut the end close to the fabric.

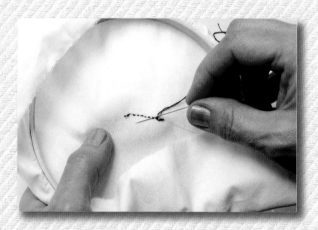

5. It is best not to continue your thread from one part of the work to another if the gap between the parts is more than 1/4" long.

French Knot

1. Insert the needle from the back, coming up on the top/right side, and pull the thread through.

2. Wrap the thread around the needle twice.

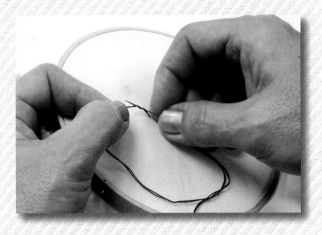

3. Pull the wraps taut, close to the fabric.

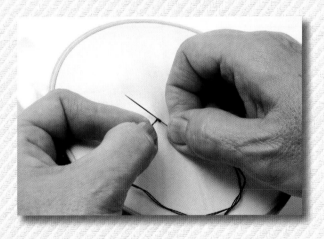

4. Insert the tip of the needle back into the fabric just a few threads from the spot where you came up.

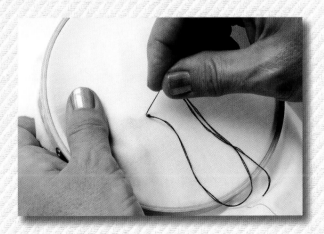

5. Pull the thread through to the back of the fabric using your fingers to help guide the thread to form a nice knot.

6. Repeat until you have all the knots you need, then tie off your thread.

Backstitch

The backstitch creates a line:

Insert your needle from the backside of the fabric through the stitching line 1/8" (point A) from the start of the line (point B) to be stitched. Pull the thread through to the top side.

Insert the needle back down at point B, under the fabric push the needle the same distance (1/8") past point A, then exit to the topside of the fabric (point C).

Insert the needle back down at point A, under the fabric push the needle the same distance (1/8") past point C, then ext to the top side of the fabric (point D).

Repeat, keeping your stitches all the same length.

Work from left to right.

Satin Stitch

1. Bring the needle up from the back just outside the left side of the space you wish to cover.

2. Crossing to the other side of the design, insert the needle just past the line, crossing back underneath to the first side and coming out right next to the first stitch.

3. Repeat this motion to completely cover the space. Your stitches will lie best if they are at a slight angle across the space rather than straight across from side to side.

4. Tie off your stitching on the back side of the block.

Lazy Daisy Stitch

1. Bring your needle up from the back side of the fabric at the inside point of the petal, pulling the thread through to the top. Insert the needle tip back down at the same spot, then back up to the top side at the rounded end of the petal (1/4" or slightly more). Wrap the thread around the needle tip.

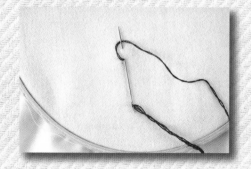

2. Pull the needle through the fabric. This forms a stitch that looks like a loop. Insert your needle back into the fabric just outside the thread, forming a tiny stitch to hold the loop in place

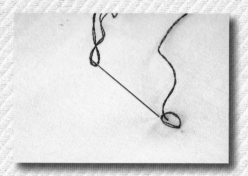

3. Pull the thread taut but not overtight. Repeat as required.

Twilling Instructions

1. Bring your needle up at 1. Take needle down at 2 and up at 3, being careful to keep the thread above the needle. Pull through, this makes a small stitch under the line.

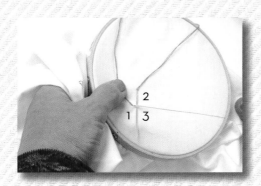

3. While holding thread down with your left thumb, pass the needle again through same stitch from top to bottom, without going through the fabric, to the right of the loop.

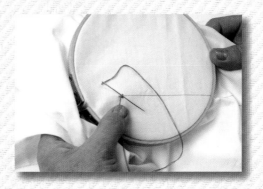

4. Pull gently to tighten and repeat as required.

2. While holding the thread down with your left thumb, pass the needle from top to bottom under the previous stitch without going through the fabric. Pull the thread through gently, do not over tighten.

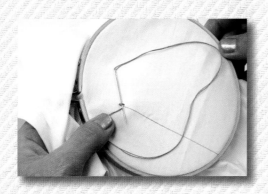

Calendar Wallhanging patterns (see pages 109-120) can also be used to make pillows.

Patterns

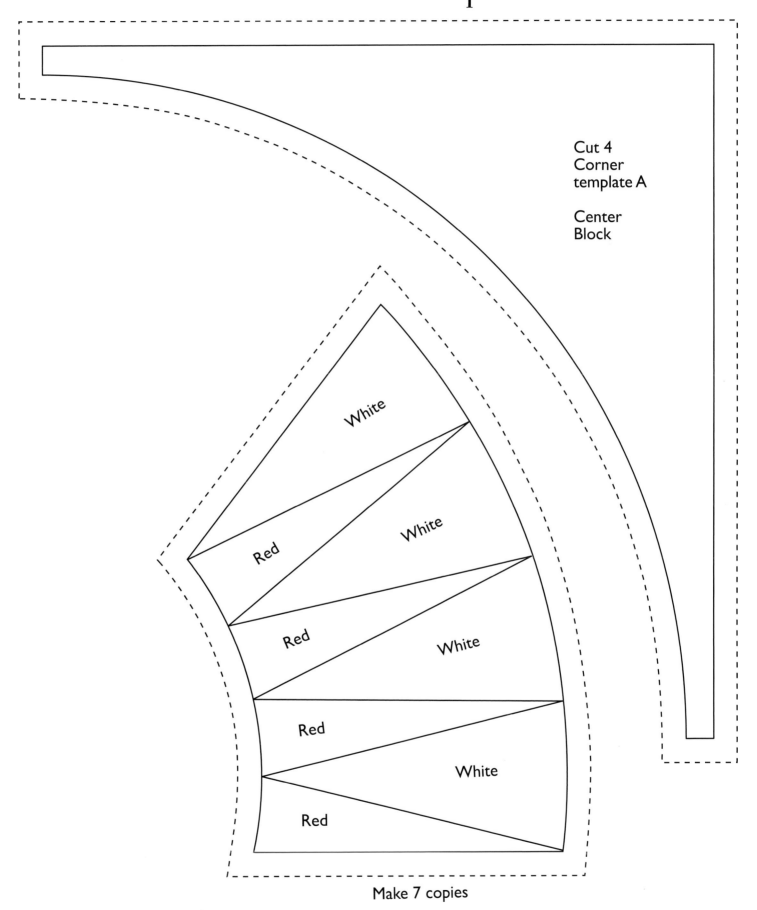

Cut 4
Corner
template A

Center
Block

White

Red

White

Red

White

Red

White

Red

Make 7 copies

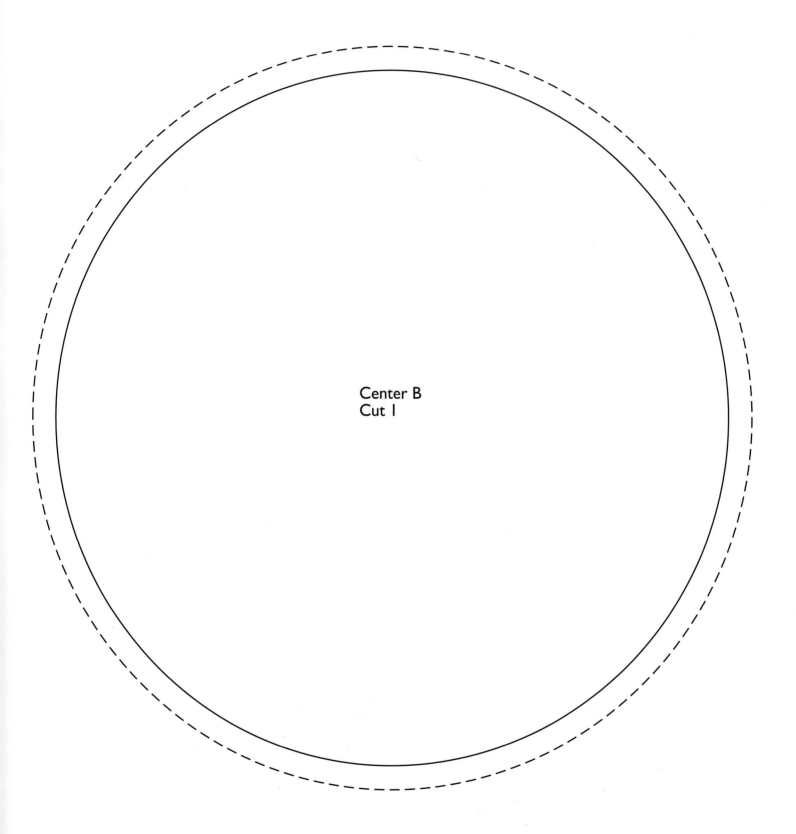

Center B
Cut 1

Embroidery pattern: Russet Bouquet

Embroidery pattern: Russet Bouquet

Embroidery pattern: Russet Bouquet

Embroidery pattern: Russet Bouquet

Embroidery pattern: Russet Bouquet

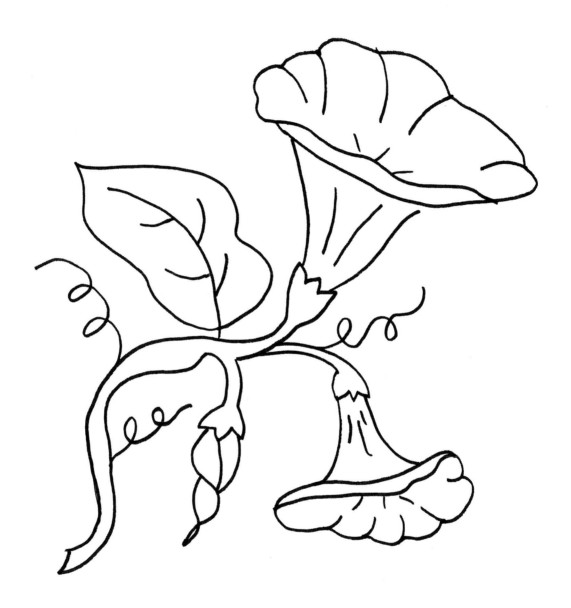

Embroidery pattern: Russet Bouquet

Center

Attach on dotted line

Embroidery pattern: Radiant Sapphire

Attach on dotted line

84

Attach on dotted line

Connect here

Stop here for
pillowcase

Embroidery pattern: Radiant Sapphire

Connect here

Attach on dotted line

Patterns: Flit and Flutter

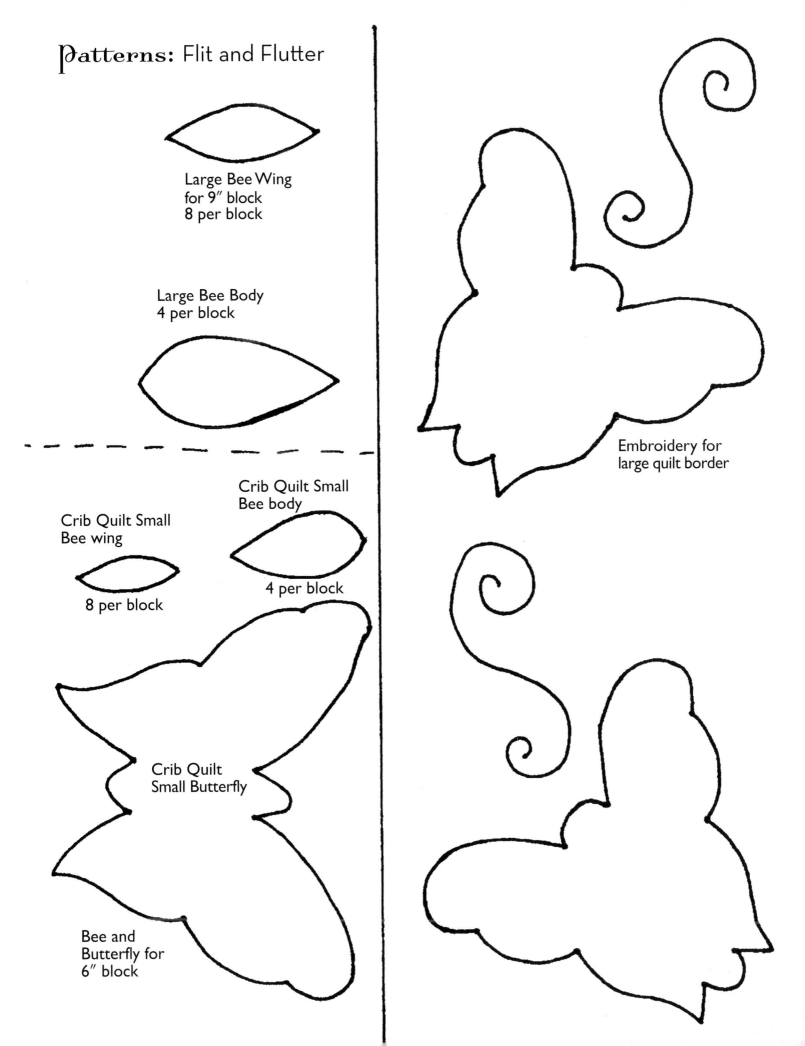

Large Bee Wing
for 9" block
8 per block

Large Bee Body
4 per block

Embroidery for
large quilt border

Crib Quilt Small
Bee body

Crib Quilt Small
Bee wing

8 per block

4 per block

Crib Quilt
Small Butterfly

Bee and
Butterfly for
6" block

Patterns: Flit and Flutter

Appliqué corner — add seam allowance on all sides

Color corner

Large
Butterfly

9″ block

The apple of
your eye......

Pr. 7:2

Embroidery pattern: Stitches of Wisdom, Bible and Candle block

Acquire wisdom! Acquire under-standing!

Proverbs 4:5

Embroidery pattern: Stitches of Wisdom, Clock block

Length of
days, years
of life,
and peace...

Pr. 3:2

Embroidery pattern: Stitches of Wisdom, Clothesline block

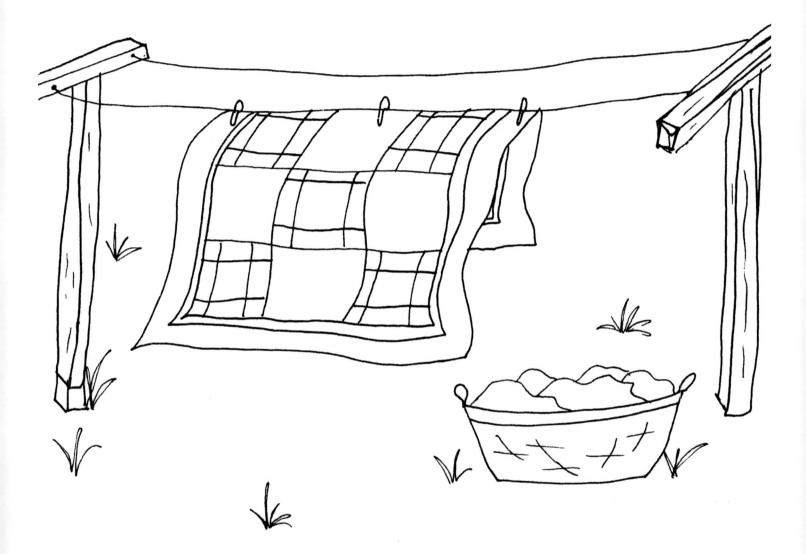

A woman who fears
the Lord shall be praised.

Pr. 31:30

Do not turn to the right or to the left.... Pr. 4:27

a garland
of
Grace...

Pr. 4:9

Honor the Lord... Pr. 3:9

Embroidery pattern: Stitches of Wisdom, Heart block

A joyful heart is good medicine...

Pr. 17:22

Embroidery pattern: Stitches of Wisdom, Pleasant Words block

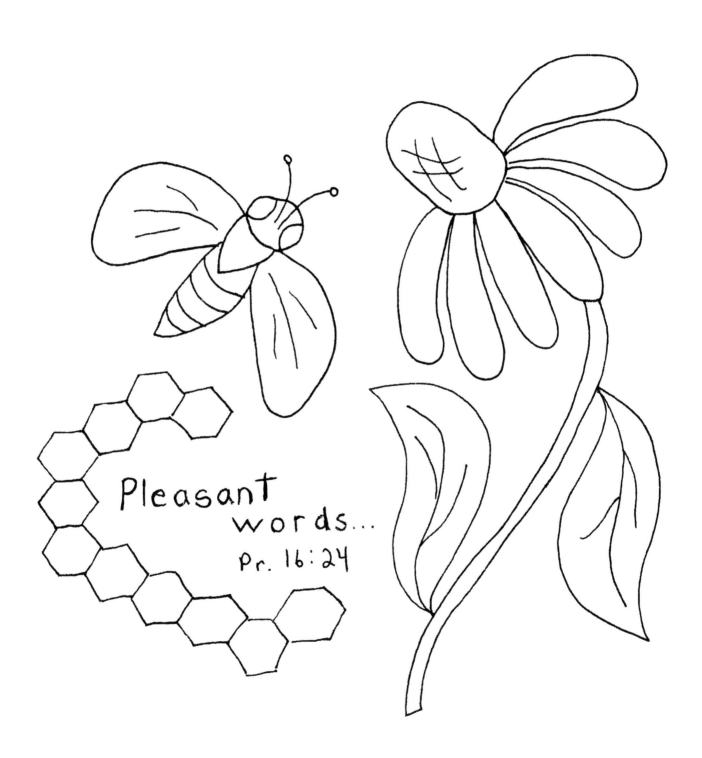

Pleasant words... Pr. 16:24

Embroidery pattern: Stitches of Wisdom,
Sunset on the Beach block

The path of the righteous
is like the light of dawn....
Pr. 4:18

Embroidery pattern: Stitches of Wisdom, Tower block

The Lord is a strong tower....

Pr. 18:10

Embroidery pattern: Stitches of Wisdom, Well block

....fresh water from

your own well......

Pr. 5:15

Outer
corner

**Embroidery
pattern:**
Vintage Daisies

Fold

Outer
border
frame

Attach on dotted line

Embroidery pattern:
Vintage Daisies

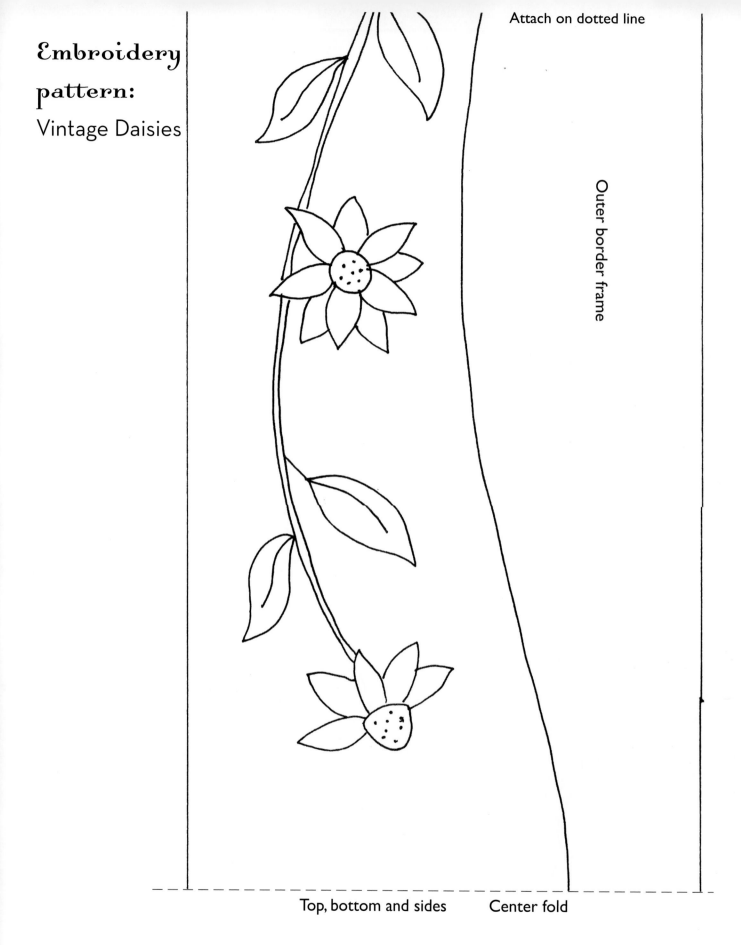

Attach on dotted line

Outer border frame

Top, bottom and sides   Center fold

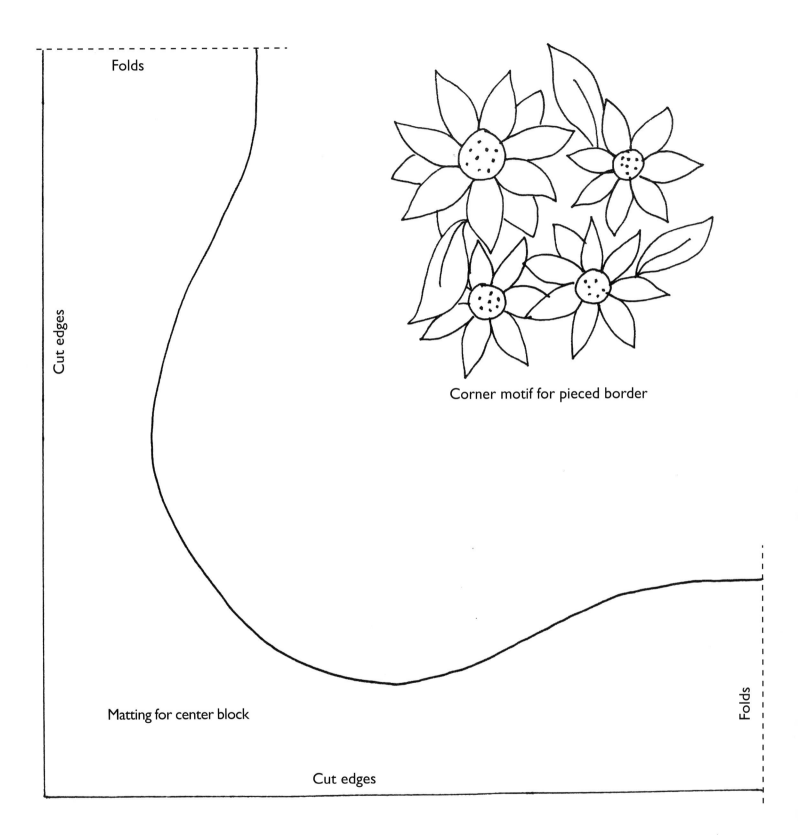

Folds

Cut edges

Matting for center block

Cut edges

Folds

Corner motif for pieced border

Embroidery pattern:

Vintage Daisies

Center__

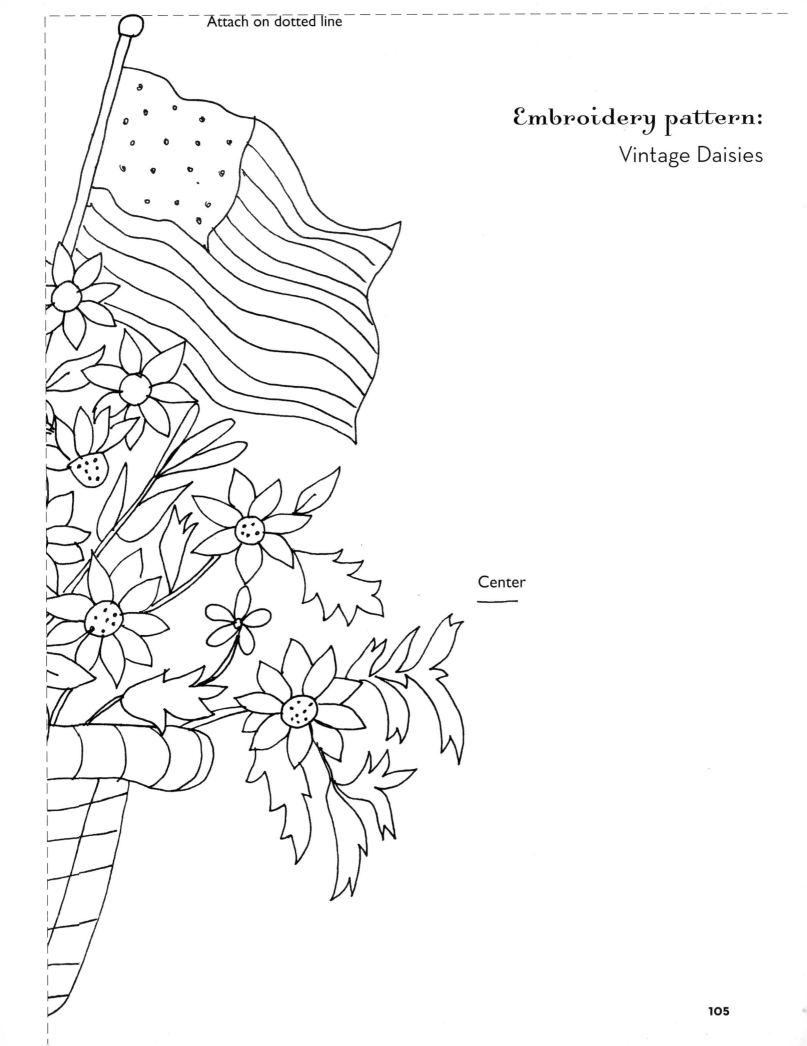

Attach on dotted line

Embroidery pattern:
Vintage Daisies

Center

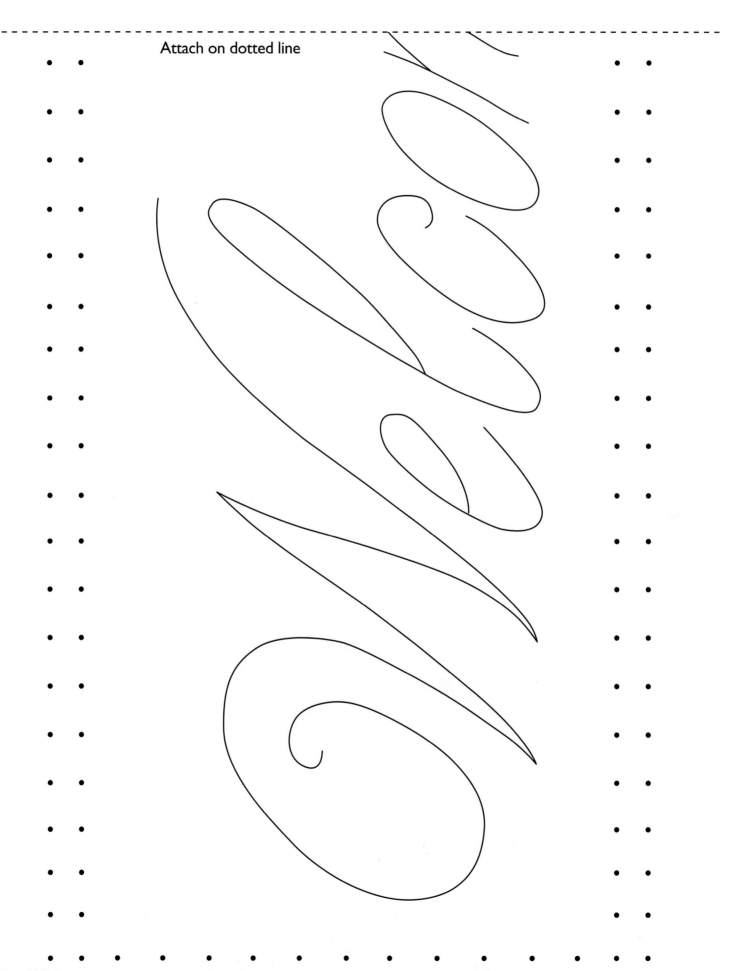

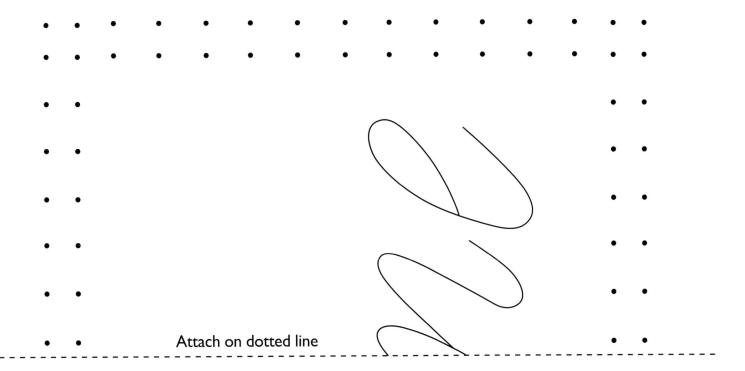

Attach on dotted line

Embroidery pattern: Bread basket liner

Bread

Embroidery pattern: All Seasons Turn Sage, Times and Seasons, & Calendar Wallhanging

Embroidery pattern: All Seasons Turn Sage, Times and Seasons, & Calendar Wallhanging

Embroidery pattern: All Seasons Turn Sage, Times and Seasons, & Calendar Wallhanging

Embroidery pattern: All Seasons Turn Sage, Times and Seasons, & Calendar Wallhanging

Embroidery pattern: All Seasons Turn Sage, Times and Seasons, & Calendar Wallhanging

Embroidery pattern: All Seasons Turn Sage, Times and Seasons, & Calendar Wallhanging

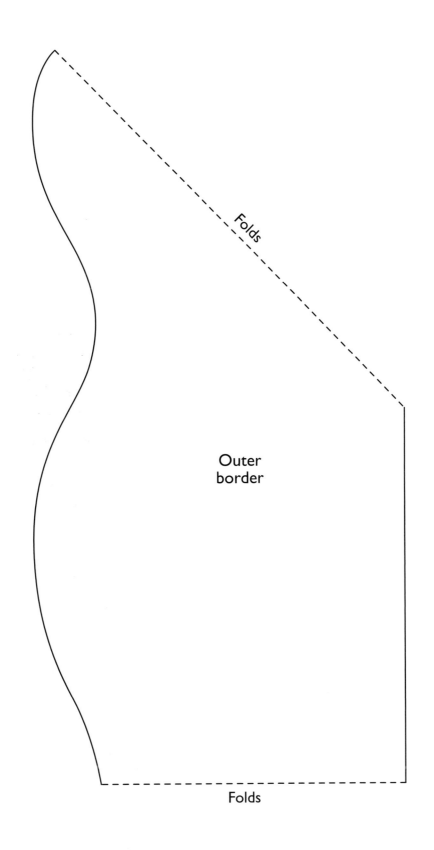

Folds

Outer
border

Folds

Other Star Books

One Piece at a Time by Kansas City Star Books – 1999

More Kansas City Star Quilts by Kansas City Star Books – 2000

Outside the Box: Hexagon Patterns from The Kansas City Star by Edie McGinnis – 2001

Prairie Flower: A Year on the Plains by Barbara Brackman – 2001

The Sister Blocks by Edie McGinnis – 2001

Kansas City Quiltmakers by Doug Worgul – 2001

O' Glory: Americana Quilts Blocks from The Kansas City Star by Edie McGinnis – 2001

Hearts and Flowers: Hand Appliqué from Start to Finish by Kathy Delaney – 2002

Roads and Curves Ahead: A Trip Through Time with Classic Kansas City Star Quilt Blocks by Edie McGinnis – 2002

Celebration of American Life: Appliqué Patterns Honoring a Nation and Its People by Barb Adams and Alma Allen – 2002

Women of Grace & Charm: A Quilting Tribute to the Women Who Served in World War II by Barb Adams and Alma Allen – 2003

A Heartland Album: More Techniques in Hand Appliqué by Kathy Delaney – 2003

Quilting a Poem: Designs Inspired by America's Poets by Frances Kite and Deb Rowden – 2003

Carolyn's Paper Pieced Garden: Patterns for Miniature and Full-Sized Quilts by Carolyn Cullinan McCormick – 2003

Friendships in Bloom: Round Robin Quilts by Marjorie Nelson and Rebecca Nelson-Zerfas – 2003

Baskets of Treasures: Designs Inspired by Life Along the River by Edie McGinnis – 2003

Heart & Home: Unique American Women and the Houses that Inspire by Kathy Schmitz – 2003

Women of Design: Quilts in the Newspaper by Barbara Brackman – 2004

The Basics: An Easy Guide to Beginning Quiltmaking by Kathy Delaney – 2004

Four Block Quilts: Echoes of History, Pieced Boldly & Appliquéd Freely by Terry Clothier Thompson – 2004

No Boundaries: Bringing Your Fabric Over the Edge by Edie McGinnis – 2004

Horn of Plenty for a New Century by Kathy Delaney – 2004

Quilting the Garden by Barb Adams and Alma Allen – 2004

Stars All Around Us: Quilts and Projects Inspired by a Beloved Symbol by Cherie Ralston – 2005

Quilters' Stories: Collecting History in the Heart of America by Deb Rowden – 2005

Libertyville: Where Liberty Dwells, There is My Country by Terry Clothier Thompson – 2005

Sparkling Jewels, Pearls of Wisdom by Edie McGinnis – 2005

Grapefruit Juice and Sugar: Bold Quilts Inspired by Grandmother's Legacy by Jenifer Dick – 2005

Home Sweet Home by Barb Adams and Alma Allen – 2005

Patterns of History: The Challenge Winners by Kathy Delaney – 2005

My Quilt Stories by Debra Rowden – 2005

Quilts in Red and Green and the Women Who Made Them by Nancy Hornback and Terry Clothier Thompson – 2006

Hard Times, Splendid Quilts: A 1930s Celebration, Paper Piecing from The Kansas City Star by Carolyn Cullinan McCormick – 2006

Art Nouveau Quilts for the 21st Century by Bea Oglesby – 2006

Designer Quilts: Great Projects from Moda's Best Fabric Artists – 2006

Birds of a Feather by Barb Adams and Alma Allen – 2006

Feedsacks! Beautiful Quilts from Humble Beginnings by Edie McGinnis – 2006

Kansas Spirit: Historical Quilt Blocks and the Saga of the Sunflower State by Jeanne Poore – 2006

Bold Improvisation: Searching for African-American Quilts – The Heffley Collection by Scott Heffley – 2007

The Soulful Art of African-American Quilts: Nineteen Bold, Improvisational Projects by Sonie Ruffin – 2007

Alphabet Quilts: Letters for All Ages by Bea Oglesby – 2007

Beyond the Basics: A Potpourri of Quiltmaking Techniques by Kathy Delaney – 2007

Golden's Journal: 20 Sampler Blocks Honoring Prairie Farm Life by Christina DeArmond, Eula Lang and Kaye Spitzli – 2007

Borderland in Butternut and Blue: A Sampler Quilt to Recall the Civil War Along the Kansas/Missouri Border by Barbara Brackman – 2007

Come to the Fair: Quilts that Celebrate State Fair Traditions by Edie McGinnis – 2007

Cotton and Wool: Miss Jump's Farewell by Linda Brannock – 2007

You're Invited! Quilts and Homes to Inspire by Barb Adams and Alma Allen, Blackbird Designs – 2007

Portable Patchwork: Who Says You Can't Take it With You? by Donna Thomas – 2008

Quilts for Rosie: Paper Piecing Patterns from the '40s by Carolyn Cullinan McCormick – 2008

Fruit Salad: Appliqué Designs for Delicious Quilts by Bea Oglesby – 2008

Red, Green and Beyond by Nancy Hornback and Terry Clothier Thompson – 2008

A Dusty Garden Grows by Terry Clothier Thompson – 2008

We Gather Together: A Harvest of Quilts by Jan Patek – 2008

With These Hands: 19th Century-Inspired Primitive Projects for Your Home by Maggie Bonanomi – 2008

As the Cold Wind Blows by Barb Adams and Alma Allen – 2008

Caring for Your Quilts: Textile Conservation, Repair and Storage by Hallye Bone – 2008

The Circuit Rider's Quilt: An Album Quilt Honoring a Beloved Minister by Jenifer Dick – 2008

Embroidered Quilts: From Hands and Hearts by Christina DeArmond, Eula Lang and Kaye Spitzli – 2008

Reminiscing: A Whimsicals Collections by Terri Degenkolb – 2008

Scraps and Shirttails: Reuse, Re-purpose and Recycle! The Art of Green Quilting by Bonnie Hunter – 2008

Queen Bees Mysteries:

Murders on Elderberry Road by Sally Goldenbaum – 2003

A Murder of Taste by Sally Goldenbaum – 2004

Murder on a Starry Night by Sally Goldenbaum – 2005

Dog-Gone Murder by Marnette Falley – 2008

Project Books:

Fan Quilt Memories by Jeanne Poore – 2000

Santa's Parade of Nursery Rhymes by Jeanne Poore – 2001

As the Crow Flies by Edie McGinnis – 2007

Sweet Inspirations by Pam Manning – 2007

Quilts Through the Camera's Eye by Terry Clothier Thompson – 2007

Louisa May Alcott: Quilts of Her Life, Her Work, Her Heart by Terry Clothier Thompson – 2008

The Lincoln Museum Quilt: A Reproduction for Abe's Frontier Cabin by Barbara Brackman and Deb Rowden – 2008

Dinosaurs - Stomp, Chomp and Roar by Pam Manning – 2008

Carrie Hall's Sampler: Favorite Blocks from a Classic Pattern Collection by Barbara Brackman – 2008

DVD Projects:

The Kansas City Stars: A Quilting Legacy – 2008

Notes: